THE U.S. ARMY
ZOMBIE

COMBAT FILES

FROM THE LOST ARCHIVES OF THE UNDEAD

DEPARTMENT OF THE ARMY

ADAM REGER

Illustrated by David Wheeler

D0089167

Guilf

An imprint of Globe Pequot

Distributed by NATIONAL BOOK NETWORK

Copyright © 2017 by Rowman & Littlefield

British Library Cataloguing in Publication Information Available

Library of Congress Cataloging-in-Publication Data Available

ISBN 978-1-4930-2939-6 (paperback)
ISBN 978-1-4930-2940-2 (e-book)

∞™ The paper used in this publication meets the minimum requirements of American
National Standard for Information Sciences—Permanence of Paper for Printed Library
Materials, ANSI/NISO Z39.48-1992.

Printed in the United States of America

TABLE OF CONTENTS

PREFACE

by Johann von Breather, Military Historian

When one considers the great American project, can it not be said that the only constant in our nation's history has been change? From a monarchy governed by a mad king an ocean away to a representative democracy, from horse-drawn carriages on cobblestone streets to electric cars on superhighways, from the Pony Express to Skype and Snapchat, our nation has continually changed and reinvented itself.

Nowhere in our society is that fact plainer than in the hallowed halls of the United States Army. While order and a sense of duty have remained constants since the founding of that fine fighting force, little else remains the same. Weaponry has advanced dramatically since the days of muskets and drummer boys. Women are now permitted to serve in various wings of the force, as are gay and lesbian soldiers. And the natty felt and wool ensembles of the Revolutionary and Civil War forces, charmingly but eclectically accessorized, have given way to jungle, desert, and Arctic camouflage.

But the prime example of the Army's ability to adapt and change is in the book you now hold in your hands. It is a story so striking and unlikely, I would never have uncovered it had it not hit me over the head.

Literally.

The story begins in Carlisle, Pennsylvania, in the archives of the U.S. War College, where I was cross-checking lists of names for a project on the heroic dishwashers and sous chefs of the Army (years 1919–1945). Kneeling down to fetch another dusty register from a low archive shelf, I must have bumped the shelf above me, for I heard a shifting of pages, the scrape of binding boards, and then felt a sharp thump at the base of my cranium, and collapsed on the dusty floor.

When I came to, I did not have to look far for the item that had concussed me. It was a simple handbook, perfect-bound, ideal for usage in the field. Though its binding was intact even after so many years, time had erased the book's title from the cover. Opening it up, I was immediately intrigued.

U.S. Army Zombie Combat Skills.

I flipped to the title page and was incredulous to see the publication date: 1949. Nearly two decades before zombies first lumbered into the popular consciousness, with George Romero's *Night of the Living Dead* in 1968. Yet here was this book, providing evidence that zombies were on the scene at a time when Americans feared not brain-eating gray creatures, but brainwashing Reds.

There must be some misunderstanding, I thought. The Army, mad for complicated acronyms, must have used "zombie" inadvertently, to stand for some zoological initiative or other, or perhaps a field operation in Zimbabwe or Zaire. Perhaps, I thought, the book had hit me harder than I first imagined.

But no. As I paged through *Combat Skills*, it became inescapably plain to me that the book was exactly what it purported to be: a guide for America's fighting men, packed with tips—and copious, practical illustrations, which you can see in this volume—on how to fight the walking, moaning dead should they ever come to plague our streets.

By the time I finished scanning the text, I knew my book on those dishwashers and prep cooks would go on the back burner, to cook forever like some godforsaken bouillabaisse. This volume would rewrite history single-handedly, contravening decades of assumptions about the nation's armed forces, dashing forever our received wisdom pertaining to our military's stance toward the undead.

I sat on the dusty floor of the archives and read until my eyes crossed, scarcely believing what I was seeing. Page after page made a mockery of my prior assumptions about the United States military.

What was most astounding, however, is the evidence of adaptability and responsiveness that I saw in the U.S. Army's ever-changing zombie policy. If you walk away from this incredible compendium before you without knowing the proper way to enter a room when zombies are in the area, how to express zombie anal sacs, or the proper conditioning techniques to use when preparing your Military Working Zombie (MWZ) for duty, it's no skin off my nose. But you must at least come away from the book knowing this: The Army has been ceaseless in its efforts to improve and optimize its zombie-focused operations. Most remarkably, this has included a wholesale shift away from the bullet-to-the-brain, kill-'em-all mentality toward zombies that was so characteristic of the Army's first operations manuals. Instead, owing to several major discoveries throughout the '70s and '80s, the Army reversed course, pulled off a complete 180, and instead of shooting for the head ordered its men to shoot to preserve zombies—those brain-eating monsters, those ceaseless nightmares—as if they were not enemy combatants, a scourge to be wiped out, but valuable assets, commodities that could be not only salvaged but put to good use.

Indeed, that is exactly how the Army came to view the great undead menace by the year 1990. Why send living, breathing soldiers, or even dogs, into a burning building to search for unconscious comrades and trapped civilians when there were perfectly good MWZs, who don't get upset at a little heat or a patch of blistered and melting skin, to go and do it for them? Why risk the lives of living men crossing a minefield when zombies could wander willy-nilly through the same field, announcing the presence of a land mine by the explosion of their limbs into fifty pieces? Why waste money on propaganda against the commies when the sight of a pack of zombies chafing against their leather leashes, hungry for those borscht- and Marx-fed brains, was enough to give the Kremlin nightmares and turn the average Ivan into a red-blooded capitalist?

You may say that it all makes so much sense, that of course the Army would follow this path—*hogwash!* Can you imagine the guts it took to even suggest rounding up a pack of zombies and keeping them on Army bases, just yards from where our boys sleep, eat, and train? Why, the very idea's crazy. There's nothing obvious or inevitable about it at all.

A bloodthirsty force, deranged by a single-minded focus on killing and total obliteration.

It sounds scary, doesn't it? But this is exactly what the U.S. Army was up against in the early 1950s, at the very dawn of the Cold War, as it crafted its policies and techniques to combat the threat posed by zombies—the walking, drooling, ceaselessly hungry undead who threatened to erupt in outbreaks of frenzied, brain-starved packs roaming unstoppably over hill and dale, city and country.

Camouflaged Soldiers

Except the problem, now that we have the historical distance to evaluate things properly, was not the zombies.

No, in fact it was the U.S. Army that was bloodthirsty, so focused on killing that it took more than 30 years before it realized the tactical asset it was squandering with every bullet to the head of a staggering, slobbering zombie.

Talk about a waste of bullets! With every kill shot the Army was declining the services of a skilled and loyal bomb-sniffing zombie. Every zombie skull shattered represented a decoy, a mine-sweeping asset, a warm body that, utilized more efficiently, could be depended upon to waste the time, confuse the senses, and scare the living daylights out of our nation's enemies.

To regard the emphasis on total warfare now is to look back on an Army so focused on destroying the thing it feared that it couldn't see the very useful nose on its own face. Killing zombies is like earlier generations of seaside folks so overrun with lobsters that they hired men to exterminate them. True enough, went the fishermen's thinking, those vermin of the sea were worth their weight in gold (and then some), but they were ugly, and what a lot of work to get the meat out!

This is the historical context one must keep in mind while leafing through these pages. *U.S. Army Zombie Combat Skills* is a handbook, an invaluable guide to the fight against zombies, but it also represents a time capsule. So sure was the Army of the righteousness of its cause, it never stopped to see the dumb, constantly moving zombie enemy as anything but carcasses to be contained, destroyed, and disposed of. So much a way of life had killing zombies become that men decorated their weapons and tanks with clever slogans, and a small sweepstakes evolved with soldiers competing in the number of "trophies"—chiefly zombie toes—they were able to collect.

But such is the enterprising, innovative spirit of the U.S. Army that they gave it a try. It is to their infinite credit that they did. They tried it out, and they learned some things—many things, in fact, which they set down in the volumes that I spent those next few months poring over.

Now, after some wangling and wrangling with the Army's legal department, I am proud to present some of the most remarkable moments of those volumes, together in one handy volume for your edification and reading pleasure.

PART I

FIGHTING THE ZOMBIE MENACE

THE LIVING
WARRIOR ETHOS

Combat with the undead is chaotic, intense, and shockingly destructive. In your first battle you will experience the confusing and often terrifying sights, sounds, smells, and dangers of the zombie battlefield—but you must learn to survive and win despite them.

You could face a fierce and relentless undead enemy.

You could be surrounded by destruction, death, and reanimated corpses.

Your leaders may shout urgent commands, lost in the drone of the advancing undead enemy.

Friendly fire rounds might impact near you.

The air could be filled with the smell of explosives, propellant, and decaying flesh.

You might hear the screams of a devoured comrade.

However, even in all this confusion and fear, remember that you are not alone. You are part of a well-trained team, backed by the most powerful combined arms force and the most modern technology in the world. You must keep faith with your fellow soldiers, remember your training, and do your duty to the best of your ability. Also remember that the enemy has no faith, no training, and only the crudest weaponry. If you do, and you uphold your Warrior Ethos, you can win and return home with honor.

This is the soldier's zombie combat field manual. It tells the soldier how to perform the combat skills needed to survive on the battlefield against the undead. All soldiers, across all branches and components, must learn these basic skills. Noncommissioned officers (NCOs) must ensure that their soldiers receive training on—and know—these vital combat skills.

A vital case study in understanding the mindset of the Army's zombie-fighting corps is the esprit de corps of the fighting men who faced the undead enemy on the ground. What was it that motivated them? How did they view the enemy—with fear, with hatred? With a determination to fight to their last breath to keep the undead menace from gaining a foothold on these shores?

The Living Warrior Ethos serves as a neat encapsulation of what the Army's zombie-fighting forces thought and believed and how they talked about zombies and the ceaseless fight against them.

LIVING WARRIOR ETHOS

What is the Living Warrior Ethos? At first glance, it is just four simple lines embedded in the Living Warrior's Creed. Yet it is the spirit represented by these four lines that:

► Compels Warriors to fight through all adversity, under any circumstances, in order to achieve victory.

► Represents the Living Warrior's loyal, tireless, and selfless commitment to his nation, his mission, his unit, his Living race, and his fellow Warriors.

► Captures the essence of combat, Army Values, and Warrior Culture.

Sustained and developed through discipline, commitment, and pride, these four lines motivate every Warrior to persevere and, ultimately, to refuse defeat. These lines go beyond mere survival. They speak to forging life over death, victory from chaos; to overcoming fear, hunger, deprivation, and fatigue; and to accomplishing the mission:

The Warrior's Creed

I am a Living American Soldier.
I am a fighter and a member of a team.
I serve the Living people of the United States
and live the Army Values.

I WILL ALWAYS PLACE THE MISSION FIRST.
I WILL NEVER ACCEPT DEFEAT.
I WILL NEVER QUIT.
I WILL NEVER LEAVE A FALLEN COMRADE.
I WILL NOT HESITATE TO TERMINATE
COMRADES BITTEN BY THE UNDEAD.

I am disciplined, physically and mentally tough, trained,
and proficient in my Warrior tasks and drills.
I always maintain my arms, my equipment, and myself.
I am an expert and I am a professional.
I stand ready to deploy, engage, and destroy the Undead
enemies of the United States of America in close combat.
I am a guardian of freedom and the American way of life.
I am a Living American Soldier.

CHAPTER 1

THE WARRIOR

From the dawn of the Army's efforts to counter the looming zombie menace, the skill and strength of the individual U.S. soldier have been central to opposing the undead. The very nature of the enemy, after all, is erratic, decentralized—impossible to prepare for strategically. Every zombie encounter is different—and yet a consistent set of tactics gradually emerged, the better to anticipate and dismantle the threat posed by zombies, whether they be roving and ravaging in clusters, swarms, pods, prides, or any other formation.

It would be difficult to imagine a more formidable task than fighting off wave after wave of zombies, then going back to base and penning reports detailing the two-person combat formations used, or proposing best practices for clearing a room under zombie occupation. The fighting men of those early anti-zombie units deserve our undying—*pun intended!*—respect for a job well done. They can scarcely be blamed for the Army's dramatic turn, some decades later, toward an ethic of preservation, salvage, and capture rather than the bellicose, two-fisted style pioneered by the soldier depicted in the chapter that follows.

—Historian's note

The Warrior

Military service is more than a "job." It is a profession with the enduring purpose to win wars and destroy the undead during a zombie uprising. The Living Warrior Ethos demands a dedication to duty that may involve

putting your life on the line, even when survival is in question, for a cause greater than yourself. As a soldier you must motivate yourself to rise above the worst battle conditions—no matter what it takes or how long it takes. That is the heart of the Warrior Ethos, which is the foundation for your commitment to victory in times of peace and war. While always exemplifying the four parts of the Warrior Ethos, you must have absolute faith in yourself and your team, as they are trained and equipped to destroy the undead in close combat. Warrior drills are a set of nine battle drills, consisting of individual tasks that develop and manifest the Warrior Ethos in soldiers.

OPERATIONAL ENVIRONMENT

1.1. This complex operational environment offers no relief or rest from contact with the undead across the spectrum of conflict. Battlefields of the Global War on Zombie-ism, and battles to be fought in the U.S. Army's future, are and will be frightening, asymmetrical, violent, unpredictable, and multidimensional. Every soldier must be ready and able to

"Kill 'em All":
The Army's Early Approach to the Undead Menace

The early days of zombie fighting were a grisly, bloodthirsty time for the United States Army, when "A bullet in the brain" and "If it's gray, we must slay" were the prevailing attitudes, as these figures demonstrate.

➤ *The colorful, freewheeling style of early zombie fighters is captured in this depiction of a soldier and his zombie-killing weapon of choice.*

➤ *Note the grisly bloodshed in this instructional figure.*

➤ *A bullet-riddled target from Army shooting practice tells the story of the Army's attitude toward the zombie enemy.*

enter combat; ready to fight—and win—against the undead, *any* time, *any* place.

LIVING LAW OF LAND WARFARE

1.2. The conduct of armed hostilities on land is regulated by Federal Mandate 27-10 and the Living Law of Land Warfare. Their purpose is to diminish the evils of war by protecting combatants *and* noncombatants from unnecessary suffering, and by safeguarding certain fundamental living human rights of those who fall into the hands of the undead, particularly undead prisoners of war, detainees, wounded and sick, and civilians.

CHAPTER 2

MEDICINE IN THE FIELD

There's no greater irony, looking back at the early years of anti-zombie combat, than comparing today's policies to the way soldiers were trained to respond to any and all injuries sustained during contact with the undead enemy.

What is ironic about treating wounded soldiers with the greatest possible care, you may well ask? Not a thing. But consider the haste and extreme care with which soldiers, beginning in the mid-1980s and early 1990s, practiced these same techniques—from applying tourniquets to stabilizing broken ankles, administering intravenous fluids, and even treating heat rashes—on the zombies themselves. From the very beginning the techniques the Army would ultimately use to protect its zombie assets were fully developed and already in use in battlefield medics' tents.

—Historian's note

Camouflaged Soldiers

Medicine in the Field

Combat casualty care is the treatment administered to a wounded soldier after he has been moved out of an engagement area or the undead have been suppressed. This level of care can help save life and limb until medical personnel arrive. Soldiers might have to depend upon their own first aid knowledge and skills to save themselves (self-aid) or another soldier (buddy aid or combat lifesaver skills). This knowledge and training can possibly save a life, prevent permanent disability, or reduce long periods of hospitalization. The only requirement is to know what to do—and what not to do—in certain instances.

Personal hygiene and preventive medicine are simple, common-sense measures that each soldier can perform to protect his health and that of others. Taking these measures can greatly reduce time lost due to disease and non-battle injury.

The Army warfighter doctrine, developed for a widely dispersed and rapidly moving battlefield, recognizes that battlefield constraints limit the number of trained medical personnel available to provide immediate, far-forward care. This section defines combat lifesaver, provides lifesaving measures (first aid) techniques, and discusses casualty evacuation.

COMBAT LIFESAVER

2.1. The role of the combat lifesaver was developed to increase far-forward care to battle. At least one member—though ideally *every* member of each squad, team, and crew—should be a trained combat lifesaver. The leader is seldom a combat lifesaver, since he will have less time to perform those duties than would another member of his unit.

2.2. So what exactly is a combat lifesaver? He is a nonmedical combat soldier. His *secondary* mission is to help the combat medic provide basic emergency care to bitten or mauled members of his squad, team, or crew, and to aid in evacuating them, mission permitting. He complements, rather than replaces, the combat medic. He receives training in enhanced first aid and selected medical procedures such as initiating intravenous uninfected blood infusions. Combat lifesaver training bridges the first aid training (self-aid or buddy aid, or SABA) given to all soldiers in basic training, and the more advanced medical training given to Medical Specialists (MOS 91W), also known as combat medics.

LIFESAVING MEASURES (FIRST AID)

2.3. When a soldier is bitten, scratched, or mauled, he must receive first aid immediately. Most injured or ill soldiers can return to their units to fight or support. This is mainly because they receive appropriate and timely first aid, followed by the best possible medical care. To help ensure this happens, every soldier should have combat lifesaver training on basic lifesaving procedures.

TABLE 2.1. First aid procedures.

1	Check for BREATHING	Lack of oxygen, due to either compromised airway or inadequate breathing, can cause brain damage or, when accompanied by zombie infection, undeath in just a few minutes. Also be wary of droning or extremely foul breath. Both are early signs of undeath that if detected require you to restrain or terminate the victim.
2	Check for BLEEDING vs OOZING	Life can continue only with sufficient blood to carry oxygen to tissues. Blood pumped through a living body can escape at an alarming rate when the victim is wounded. When dressing a wound, however, pay close attention: if the wound begins to ooze instead of bleed, or if the area around the wound begins to bubble and spread, these are signs of zombie-ism, and you must act accordingly, either applying a tourniquet or terminating the victim.
3	Check for SHOCK	Unless shock is prevented, first aid performed, and medical treatment provided, undeath may result in an infected victim, even with an otherwise nonfatal injury. Note that the first signs of shock are also the first signs of zombie-ism: slow reflexes, drool, glazed or hollow eyes, low body temp, and clammy skin, and thus it can be hard to decipher between shock and early undeath. Proceed with caution.

Check for Breathing

2.4. Check first to see if the casualty's heart is beating, then to see if he is breathing. This paragraph discusses what to do in each possible situation.

React to Stoppage of Heartbeat

2.5. If a casualty's heart stops beating, you must both immediately seek medical help and be prepared to fight or terminate your infected comrade. The window between dead and undead closes fast. You must move quickly in this gap of time to save your fellow soldier—for if you can't save him, he will become undead and require termination. Thus, *seconds count!* Stoppage of the heart is soon followed by cessation of respiration, unless that has already happened. Remain calm, but think first, and act quickly.

Assess and Position Casualty

2.6. To assess the casualty, do the following:

1. *Check* for responsiveness. Establish whether the casualty is conscious by gently shaking him and asking, "Are you OK?"

2. *Call* for help, if appropriate.

3. *Position* the unconscious casualty so that he is lying on his back and on a firm surface.

Open Airway of Unconscious or Nonbreathing Casualty

2.7. The tongue is the single most common airway obstruction. In most cases just using the head-tilt/chin-lift technique can clear the airway. This pulls the tongue away from the air passage.

Early Forays into Zombie Life-Saving

A curious feature of the Army's remarkable shift in zombie policy is the many hints of what was to come. As evidence, consider these illustrations of lifesaving techniques applied to the undead.

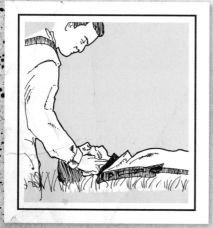

> One really has to wonder how long the soldier pictured waited while checking for this zombie's pulse.

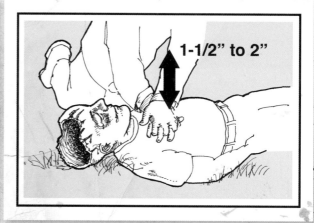

1-1/2" to 2"

> The fact that this zombie's empty brain cavity is clearly exposed might suggest chest compression would be unnecessary, but apparently not.

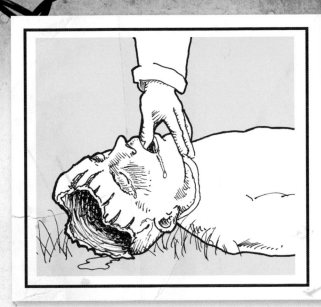

>In light of the Army's early "kill 'em all" policies, it may be incredible how little thought was given to soldiers' safety when dealing with undead combatants, as in this image . . .

>. . . or this one . . .

>. . . or, especially, this rather remarkable image. I mean, how is that safe?!

Although the head-tilt/chin-lift technique is an important procedure in opening the airway, take extreme care with it, because while you are trying to save a comrade, it may already be too late and thus you are in close quarters with a zombie. Proceed with caution. Watch for yellowing of the teeth, dilated eyes, or peeling or bubbling skin. If you note any of these symptoms, cease all contact with the wounded's mouth. Furthermore, using too much force while performing this maneuver can cause more spinal injury. In a casualty with a suspected neck injury or severe head trauma, the safest approach to opening the airway is the jaw-thrust technique because, in most cases, you can do it without extending the casualty's neck.

WARNING

Avoid pressing too deeply into the soft tissue under the casualty's chin, because you might obstruct his airway.

2.8. Call for help, and then position the casualty. Move (roll) him onto his back. Perform a finger sweep. If you see foreign material or vomit in the casualty's mouth, promptly remove it, but avoid spending much time doing so. Open the airway using the jaw-thrust or head-tilt/chin-lift technique.

Check for Breathing while Maintaining Airway

1. *Look* for his chest to rise and fall. Watch for unusual amounts of drool.

2. *Listen* for sound of breathing by placing your ear near his mouth. Listen close: Moaning is an early sign of zombie-ism.

3. *Feel* for the flow of air on your cheek. Breath should be clean, clear, fresh. Bad breath is a bad sign.

4. *Perform* rescue breathing if he fails to resume breathing spontaneously and there are no signs of zombie-ism.

Note: If the casualty resumes breathing, monitor and maintain the open airway. Ensure that he is transported to a lockdown medical treatment facility as soon as possible. Although the casualty might be trying to breathe, his airway might still be obstructed. If so, open his airway (remove the obstruction) and keep the airway open (maintain his airway).

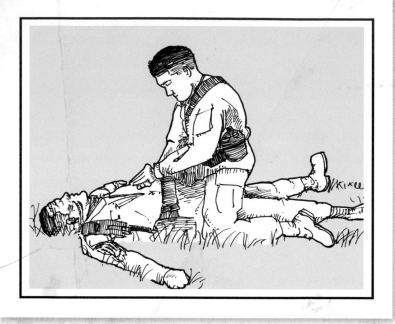

Perform Rescue Breathing or Artificial Respiration

2.9. If the casualty fails to promptly resume adequate spontaneous breathing after the airway is open, you must start rescue breathing (artificial respiration, or mouth-to-mouth). Remain calm and armed, but think and act quickly. The sooner you start rescue breathing, the more likely you are to restore his breathing. If you are not sure if the casualty is breathing, give him artificial respiration anyway.

Use Mouth-to-Mouth Method

2.10. In this best-known method of rescue breathing, inflate the casualty's lungs with air from yours. You can do this by blowing air into his mouth. If the casualty is not breathing, place your hand on his forehead and pinch his nostrils together with the thumb and index finger of the hand in use. It is best to do this under armed supervision since this is the last step before the casualty becomes undead.

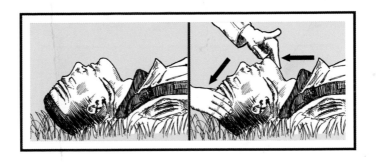

Use Mouth-to-Nose Method

2.11. Use this method if you cannot perform mouth-to-mouth rescue breathing. Normally, the reason you cannot is that the casualty has a severe jaw fracture or mouth wound or because his jaws are tightly closed by spasms, or in the early stages of undeath the casualty's incisors have extended and breath is foul. The mouth-to-nose method is the same as the mouth-to-mouth method, except that you blow into the *nose* while you hold the *lips* closed, keeping one hand at the chin. Then you remove your mouth to let the casualty exhale passively. You might have to separate the casualty's lips to allow the air to escape during exhalation. Leave it!

Determine Degree of Obstruction

2.12. A complete obstruction (no air exchange) is indicated if the casualty cannot speak, breathe, or cough at all. He might clutch his neck and move erratically. In an unconscious casualty, a complete obstruction is also indicated if, after opening his airway, you cannot ventilate him.

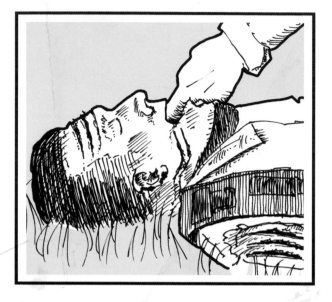

➤ *Repeat the sequence of chest thrust, finger sweep, and rescue breathing as long as necessary to clear the object from the obstructed airway.*

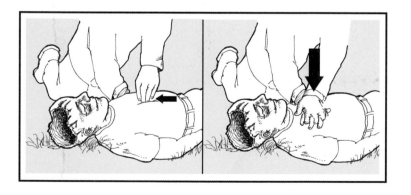

If you still cannot administer rescue breathing due to an airway obstruction, remove the obstruction:

1. Place the casualty on his back, face up.

2. Turn him all at once (avoid twisting his body).

3. Call for help.

4. Perform finger sweep.

5. Keep him face up.

6. Use the tongue-jaw lift to open his mouth.

7. Open his mouth by grasping both his tongue and lower jaw between your thumb and fingers, and lift. Again, listen for groaning and watch for excessive drool and extended incisors. Abort efforts at the first signs of zombie-ism.

8. If you cannot open his mouth, cross your fingers and thumb (crossed-finger method), and push his teeth apart. To do this, press your thumb against his upper teeth and your finger against his lower teeth.

9. Insert the index finger of your other hand down along the Inside of his cheek to the base of his tongue. Use a hooking motion from the side of the mouth toward the center to dislodge the foreign body.

Check for Bleeding

Stop Bleeding and Protect Wound

2.13. The longer a soldier bleeds from a major wound, the less likely he will survive it. You must promptly stop the external bleeding without infecting yourself. If zombie blood (Z-positive) enters your body through a cut or cavity, you will become undead. Use extreme caution.

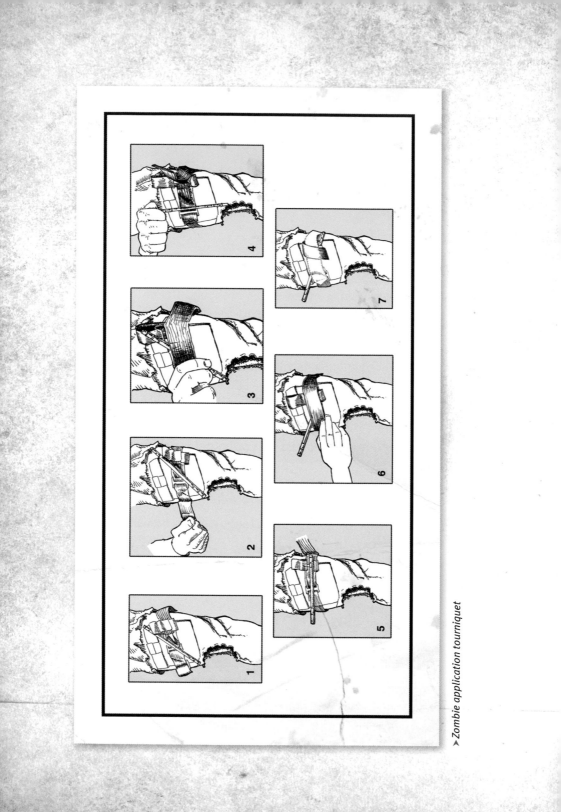

> *Zombie application tourniquet*

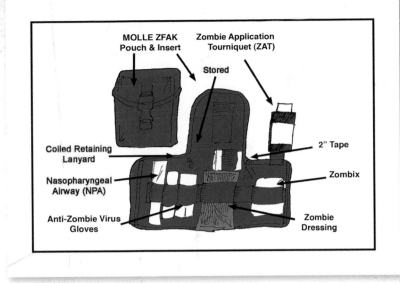

➤ *Improved zombie first aid kit*

Entrance and Exit Wounds

2.14. Before applying the dressing, carefully examine the casualty to determine if there is more than one wound. The wounds discussed here are caused by weapons. Wounds caused by bites and scratches that lead to infection will be discussed later. A stick or stake may have entered at one point and exited at another point. An exit wound is usually *larger* than its entrance wound.

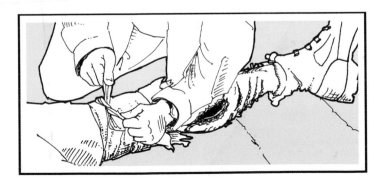

➤ *Tourniquet above knee*

2.15. Remove the casualty's field dressing from the wrapper, and grasp the tails of the dressing with both hands.

Pulling Dressing Open

2.16. Wrap the other tail in the opposite direction until the rest of the dressing is covered. The tails should seal the sides of the dressing to keep foreign material from getting under it. Tie the tails into a nonslip knot over the outer edge of the dressing. *Do not tie the knot over the wound.* In order to allow uninfected or Z-negative blood to flow to the rest of the injured limb, tie the dressing firmly enough to prevent it from slipping but without causing a tourniquet effect. That is, the skin beyond the injury should not become cool, blue, or numb.

Manual Pressure

2.17. If bleeding continues after you apply the sterile field dressing, apply direct pressure to the dressing for 5 to 10 minutes. If the casualty is conscious and can follow instructions, you can ask him to do this himself. Elevate an injured limb slightly above the level of the heart to reduce the bleeding.

2.18. If the bleeding stops, check for shock and then give first aid for that as needed. If the bleeding continues, apply a pressure dressing.

Pressure Dressing

2.19. If bleeding continues after you apply a field dressing, direct pressure, and elevation, then you must apply a pressure dressing. This helps the blood clot, and it compresses the open blood vessel. Place a wad of padding on top of the field dressing directly over the wound. Keep the injured extremity elevated.

Note: *Improvise bandages from strips of cloth such as T-shirts, socks, or other garments.*

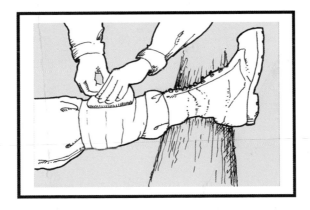

➤ *Wad of padding on top of field dressing*

2.20. Place an improvised dressing (or cravat, if available) over the wad of padding. Wrap the ends tightly around the injured limb, covering the original field dressing.

2.21. Tie the ends together in a nonslip knot, directly over the wound site. *Do not* tie so tightly that it has a tourniquet-like effect. If bleeding continues and all other measures fail, or if the limb is severed, then apply a tourniquet, but do so *only as a last resort*. When the bleeding stops, check for shock and give first aid for that, if needed.

2.22. Check fingers and toes periodically for adequate circulation. Finger- and toenails that are turning long and yellow may be an early sign of undeath. Loosen the dressing if the extremity becomes cool, blue, or numb. If bleeding continues and all other measures fail—application of dressings, covering of wound, direct manual pressure, elevation of limb above heart level, application of pressure dressing while maintaining limb elevation—then apply digital pressure.

Digital Pressure

2.23. Use this method when you are having a hard time controlling bleeding, before you apply a pressure dressing, or where pressure dressings are unavailable. Keep the limb elevated and direct pressure on the wound. At the same time press your fingers, thumbs, or whole hand where a main artery supplying the wounded area lies near the surface or over bone. This might help shut off, or at least slow, the flow of blood from the heart to the wound.

Tourniquet

2.24. A tourniquet is a constricting band placed around an arm or leg to control bleeding. A soldier whose arm or leg has been completely amputated or infected might not be yellowed, bubbling, bleeding, or suppurating when first discovered, but you should apply a tourniquet anyway. The body initially stops bleeding by contracting or clotting the blood vessels. However, when the vessels relax, or if a clot is knocked loose when the casualty is moved, the bleeding can restart. Bleeding from a major artery of the thigh, lower leg, or arm, and bleeding from multiple arteries, both of which occur in a traumatic amputation, might be more than you can control with manual pressure. If even under firm hand pressure the dressing gets soaked with blood, and if the wound continues to bleed, then you *must* apply a tourniquet.

Zombie Application Tourniquet

The ZAT is packaged for one-handed use. Slide the wounded extremity through the loop of the ZAT tape.

Position the ZAT 2 inches above a bleeding, yellowing, suppurating site that is above the knee or elbow. Pull the free running end of the tape tight, and fasten it securely back on itself.

Improvised Tourniquet

2.25. In the absence of a specially designed tourniquet, you can make one from any strong, pliable material such as gauze or muslin bandages, clothing, or cravats. Use your improvised tourniquet with a rigid, stick-like object. To minimize skin damage, the improvised tourniquet must be at least 2 inches wide.

2.26. To position the makeshift tourniquet, place it around the limb, between the wound and the body trunk, or between the wound and the heart. *Never* place it directly over a wound, a fracture, or joint. For maximum effectiveness, place it on the upper arm or above the knee on the thigh.

Application

2.27. Tie a full-knot over the stick, and twist the stick until the tourniquet tightens around the limb or the bright red bleeding stops. In the case of amputation, dark oozing blood may continue for a short time. This is the infected Z-positive blood trapped in the area between the wound and tourniquet.

2.28. You can use other means to secure the stick. Just make sure the material remains wound around the stick and that no further injury is

CAUTION

Do not remove a tourniquet yourself. Only trained medical personnel may adjust or otherwise remove or release the tourniquet, and then only in the appropriate setting. Removing a tourniquet suddenly can result in an explosion of infected blood squirting in every direction, contaminating the environment and putting others at risk.

possible. If possible, save and transport any severed (amputated) limbs or body parts with (but out of sight of) the casualty. Never cover the tourniquet. Leave it in full view. If the limb is missing (has been completely torn or gnawed off), apply a dressing to the stump. All wounds should have a dressing to protect the wound from contamination. Mark the casualty's forehead with a "T" and the time to show that he has a tourniquet. If necessary, use the casualty's blood to make this mark. Check and treat for shock, and then seek medical aid.

SHOCK

2.29. The term *shock* means various things. In medicine it means a collapse of the body's cardiovascular system, including an inadequate supply of blood to the body's tissues. Shock stuns and weakens the living body. Shock is the first phase of undeath. When the normal blood flow in the body is upset, undeath can result. Early recognition and proper first aid may save the casualty's life.

Causes and Effects of Shock

2.30. The two basic effects of shock are:

- Heart is damaged and fails to pump.

- Blood loss (heavy bleeding) depletes fluids in the vascular system.

2.31. Shock might be caused by:

- Significant loss of blood.

- Reaction to sight of a flesh wound, blood, pus, or other traumatic scene.

- Traumatic injuries.

- Burns.

- Bites or torn-off or gnawed-off limbs.

- Penetrating wounds such as from teeth, stick, nailed-through two-by-four.

Signs and Symptoms of Shock and Early Undeath

- Sweaty but cool (clammy) skin.

- No pulse.

- Pale, gray, chalky skin tone.

- Cyanosis (blue) and blotchy, peeling, or bubbling skin, especially around the mouth and lips.

- Significant loss of blood.

- Confusion or disorientation. Moving with hands extended, limping.

- Nausea, vomiting, or both.

- Bad breath.

Casualty Position

2.32. *Never* move the casualty, or his limbs, if you suspect he has fractures and they have not yet been splinted. If you have cover and the situation permits, move the casualty to cover. Lay him on his back. A casualty in shock from a flesh wound or who is having trouble breathing might breathe easier sitting up. If so, let him sit up, but monitor him carefully in case his condition worsens. Elevate his feet higher than the level of his heart. Support his feet with a stable object, such as a field pack or rolled-up clothing, to keep them from slipping off.

Casualty Evacuation

2.33. Transport by litter is safer and more comfortable for a casualty than manual carries. It is also easier for you as the bearer(s). However, manual transportation might be the only feasible method, due to the terrain or combat situation. You might have to do it to save a life. As soon as you can, transfer the casualty to a litter as soon as you find or can improvise one.

Manual Carries

2.34. When you carry a casualty manually, you must handle him carefully and correctly to prevent more serious or possibly fatal injuries. Situation permitting, organize the transport of the casualty, and avoid rushing. Perform each movement as deliberately and gently as possible. Manual carries are tiring and can increase the severity of the casualty's injury, but might be required to save his life. Two-man carries are preferred, because they provide more comfort to the casualty, are less likely to aggravate his injuries, and are less tiring for the bearers. How far you can carry a casualty depends on many factors, such as:

- Nature of the casualty's injuries.

- Your (the bearer's or bearers') strength and endurance.

- Weight of the casualty.

- Obstacles encountered during transport (natural or man-made).

- Type of terrain.

- Pursuit by the undead.

One-Man Carries

2.35. Use these carries when only one bearer is available to transport the casualty:

Fireman's Carry

2.36. This is one of the easiest ways for one person to carry another. After an unconscious or disabled casualty has been properly positioned (rolled onto his abdomen), raise him from the ground and then support him and place him in the carrying position. Here's what you do:

1. Position the casualty by rolling him onto his abdomen and straddle him. Extend your hands under his chest and lock them together.

2. Lift him to his knees as you move backward.

3. Continue to move backward, straightening his legs and locking his knees.

4. Walk forward, bringing him to a standing position. Tilt him slightly backward to keep his knees from buckling.

5. Keep supporting him with one arm, and then free your other arm, quickly grasp his wrist, and raise his arm high. Immediately pass your head under his raised arm, releasing the arm as you pass under it.

Fireman's carry

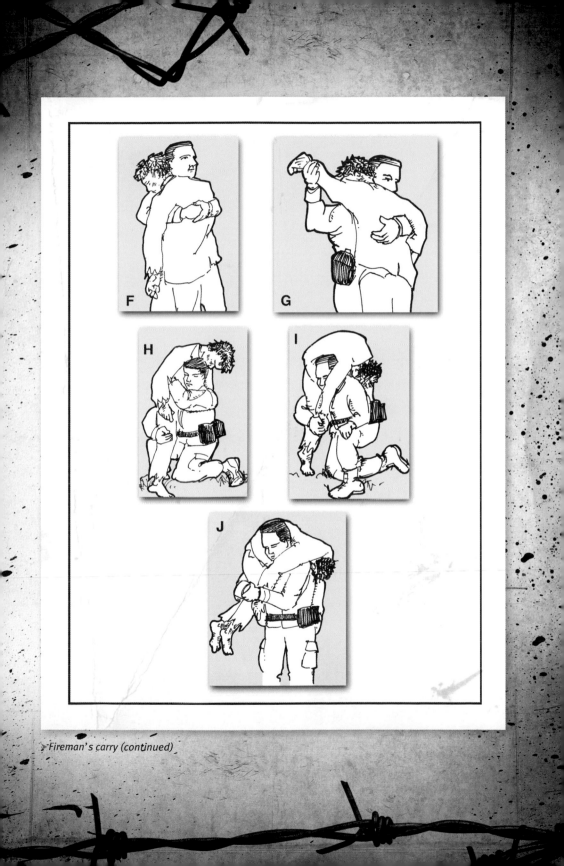

Fireman's carry (continued)

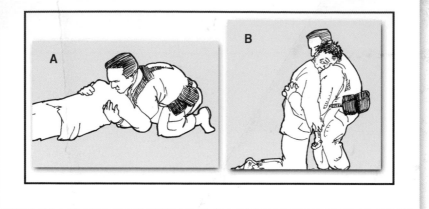

>*Alternate fireman's carry*

6. Move swiftly to face the casualty and secure your arms around his waist. Immediately place your foot between his feet, and spread them apart about 6 to 8 inches.

7. Grasp the casualty's wrist, and raise his arm high over your head.

8. Bend down and pull the casualty's arm over and down on your shoulder, bringing his body across your shoulders. At the same time, pass your arm between his legs.

9. Grasp the casualty's wrist with one hand, and place your other hand on your knee for support.

10. Rise with the casualty positioned correctly. Your other hand should be free.

WARNING

Avoid using this carry if the casualty has a devoured arm.

Danger

Unless there is an immediate life-threatening situation (such as a burning meteorite or nuclear power explosion), NEVER move a casualty who has a suspected back or neck injury. Instead, seek medical personnel for guidance on how to transport him.

MENTAL HEALTH AND MORALE

2.37. To maintain mental health and self-confidence:

Mental Hygiene

2.38. The way you think affects the way you act. If you know your job, you will probably act quickly and effectively. If you are uncertain or doubtful of your ability to do your job, you may hesitate and make wrong decisions. Positive thinking is a necessity. You must enter combat with absolute confidence in your ability to do your job. Keep in mind:

A. Fear is a basic human emotion. It is mental and physical. In itself, fear is not shameful, if controlled. It can even help you, by making you more alert and more able to do your job. For example, a fear-induced adrenaline rush might help you respond and defend yourself or your comrades quickly during an unpredicted event or combat situation. Therefore, fear can help you—use it to your advantage.

B. Avoid letting your imagination and fear run wild. Dismiss urban legends and most horror movies. They are not real. Combat, however, is real. Also remember, you are not alone. You are part of a team. Other soldiers are nearby, even though you cannot always see them. Everyone must help each other and depend on each other.

C. Worry undermines the body, dulls the mind, and slows thinking and learning. It adds to confusion, magnifies troubles, and causes you to imagine things that really do not exist. If you are worried about something, talk to your leader about it. He might be able to help solve the problem.

D. You might have to fight in any part of the world and in all types of terrain. Therefore, adjust your mind to accept conditions as they are. If mentally prepared for it, you should be able to fight under almost any conditions.

EXERCISE

2.39. Exercise your muscles and joints to maintain your physical fitness and good health. Strength is a powerful weapon against the undead, which are persistent but physically weak. Without exercise, you might lack the physical stamina and ability to fight. Physical fitness includes a healthy body, the capacity for skillful and sustained performance, the ability to recover from exertion rapidly, the desire to complete a designated task, and the confidence to face any possible event. Your own safety, health, and life may depend on your physical fitness. During lulls in combat, counteract inactivity by exercising. This helps keep your muscles and body functions ready for the next period of combat. It also helps pass the time.

REST

2.40. Just as your undead enemies return each morning to their graves to recharge, you too must rest. Your body needs regular periods of rest to restore physical and mental vigor. When you are tired, your body functions are like those of the undead—sluggish—and your ability to react is slower than normal, which makes you more susceptible to sickness and to making errors that could endanger you or others. For the best health you should get 6 to 8 hours of uninterrupted sleep each day. As that is seldom possible in combat, use rest periods and off-duty time to rest or sleep. Never be ashamed to say that you are tired or sleepy. However, *never* sleep on duty.

CHAPTER 3

FIGHTING POSITIONS

The following chapter, on fighting positions and defensive strategies when engaging the undead enemy, is vintage U.S. Army: thoroughly thought-out, field-tested, and subsequently drilled into the heads of new recruits and old sergeants alike.

While little has changed in the protocols taught to soldiers new to the business of fighting the undead, you'll note throughout this chapter the small tweaks and adjustments that have cropped up over the intervening decades. Rather than positioning oneself to blow zombies away, solo combat postures today emphasize rapid Military Working Zombie (MWZ) recovery, including addressing such concerns as keeping zombies from falling off cliffs or incurring further damage, and even being in position to quickly demobilize wounded zombies before they can do themselves further damage. After all—that's Army property now.

While life in the military is largely about falling in line and doing what one is told, not every veteran zombie-fighter has been happy about the changes to U.S. zombie-fighting protocol. Lieutenant G. Romero, of the Fighting 91st, wondered aloud at a recent regimental reunion, "What's next? The boys are gonna keep lollipops on hand in case one of them zombie bastards falls down? Next I suppose you're going to tell me they'll be expected to kiss zombie boo-boos and make it all better."

—Historian's note

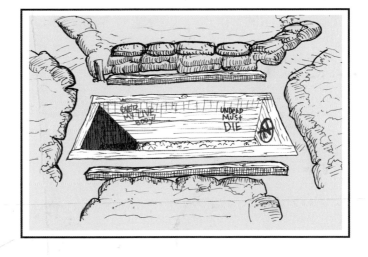

FIGHTING POSITIONS

Whether your unit is in a defensive perimeter or on an ambush line, you must seek cover from attacks and concealment from observation. From the time you prepare and occupy a fighting position, you should continue to improve it. How far you get depends on how much time you have, regardless of whether it is a hasty position or a well-prepared one with overhead cover (OHC). This chapter discusses:

- Cover and concealment.

- Sectors and fields of fire.

- Hasty and deliberate fighting positions.

COVER

3.1. To get this protection in the defense, build a fighting position to add to the natural cover afforded by the terrain. The cover of your fighting

> *Man-made cover*

position will protect you from heaved rocks and friendly fire fragments, and place a greater thickness of shielding material or earth between you and the blast wave of nuclear reactors or a meteorite's radiation, two scenarios during which zombies are likely.

3.2. Three different types of cover—overhead, frontal, and flank/rear cover—are used to make fighting positions. In addition, positions can be connected by tunnels and trenches. These allow soldiers to move between positions for engagements or resupply, while remaining protected.

Overhead Cover

3.3. Your completed position should have OHC, which enhances survivability by protecting you from indirect fire and fragmentation.

Frontal Cover

3.4. Your position needs frontal cover to protect you from crude projectiles to the front. Frontal cover allows you to fire to the oblique, as well as to hide your muzzle flash.

Flank and Rear Cover

3.5. When used with frontal and overhead cover, flank and rear cover protects you from direct undead attack and friendly fire. Natural frontal cover such as rocks, trees, logs, and rubble is best, because it is hard for the undead to detect. When natural cover is unavailable, use the dirt you remove to construct the fighting position. You can improve the effectiveness of dirt as a cover by putting it in sandbags. Fill them only three-quarters full.

➤ *Cover*

Built-Down Overhead Cover

3.6. This should not exceed 12 inches (30 centimeters). This lowers the profile of the fighting position, which aids in avoiding detection. Unlike a built-up OHC, a built-down OHC has a firing platform for elbows. You must construct a firing platform in the natural terrain upon which to rest your elbows. The firing platform will allow the use of the natural ground surface as a grazing fire platform.

HASTY AND DELIBERATE FIGHTING POSITIONS

3.7. The two types of fighting positions are hasty and deliberate. Which you construct depends on the time and equipment available and the required level of protection. Fighting positions are designed and constructed to protect you and your weapon system.

Hasty Fighting Position

3.8. Hasty fighting positions, used when there is little time for preparation, should be behind whatever cover is available. However, the term hasty does not mean that there is no digging. If a natural hole or ditch is available, use it. This position should give frontal cover from objects lobbed by the undead but allow firing to the front and the oblique. Any crater 2 to 3 feet (0.61 to 1 meter) wide offers immediate cover (except for overhead) and concealment. Digging a steep face on the side toward the undead creates a hasty fighting position. A skirmisher's trench is a shallow position that provides a hasty prone fighting position. When you need immediate shelter from undead attack, and there are no defilade firing positions available, lie prone or on your side, scrape the soil with an entrenching tool, and pile the soil in a low parapet between yourself and the undead. In all but the hardest ground, you can use this technique to quickly form a shallow, body-length pit. Orient the trench so it is oblique to the undead. This keeps your silhouette low and offers some protection from heaved objects. Some guidelines to keep in mind when operating from a hasty fighting position:

A. Make maximum use of available cover and concealment.

B. Avoid firing over cover; when possible, fire around it.

C. Avoid silhouetting against light-colored buildings, the skyline, and so on.

D. Carefully select a new fighting position before leaving an old one.

E. Avoid setting a pattern. Fire from both barricaded and non-barricaded windows.

F. Keep exposure time to a minimum.

G. Do not fire at close range without cover for your eyes, nose, and mouth to prevent infection.

H. Begin improving your hasty position immediately after occupation.

I. Do not touch anything that has been drooled, bled, or suppurated upon by the undead.

J. Use construction material that is readily available in an urban
area.

Remember: *Positions that provide cover at ground level may not provide cover on higher floors.*

Deliberate Fighting Position

3.9. Deliberate fighting positions are modified hasty positions prepared during periods of relaxed undead pressure. Your leader will assign the sectors of fire for your position's weapon system before preparation begins. Small holes are dug for automatic rifle bipod legs, so the rifle is as close to ground level as possible. Continued improvements are made to strengthen the position during the period of occupation. Improvements include adding OHC, digging grenade sumps (explained later), adding trenches to adjacent positions, and maintaining camouflage.

Table 3.1. Construction of two-man fighting position.

Parapets	Overhead Cover
Enable you to engage the undead within your assigned sector of fire. *Provide* you with protection from directly hurled objects (sticks, heads, cats). Construct parapets— *Thickness:* Minimum 39 inches (1 m) (length of M16 rifle). *Height:* 10 to 12 inches (25 to 30 centimeters) (length of a bayonet) to the front, flank, and rear.	*Protects* you from indirectly hurled objects. Your leaders will identify requirements for additional OHC based on threat capabilities. *Thickness:* Minimum 18 inches (46 cm) (length of open entrenching tool). *Concealment:* Use enough to make your position undetectable.

Two-Man Fighting Position

3.10. Prepare a two-man position in four stages. Your leader must inspect the position at each stage before you may move to the next stage.

Stage 1

3.11. Establish sectors and decide whether to build OHC up or down. Your fearless leaders must consider the factors of the mission, enemy, terrain, troops and equipment, time available, and civil considerations (METT-TC) in order to make a decision on the most appropriate fighting position to construct. For example, due to more open terrain your leader may decide to use built-down OHC. To do so, use the following procedures:

A. Check fields of fire from the prone position.

B. Assign sector of fire (primary and secondary).

C. Emplace sector stakes (right and left) to define your sectors of fire. Sector stakes prevent accidental firing into friendly positions. Items such as tent poles, metal pickets, wooden stakes, oars, tree branches, or sandbags will all make good sector stakes. The sector stakes must be sturdy and stick out of the ground at least 18 inches (46 centimeters); this will prevent your weapon from being pointed out of your sector.

D. Emplace aiming and limiting stakes to help you fire into dangerous approaches at night and at other times when visibility is poor. Forked tree limbs about 12 inches (30 centimeters) long make good stakes. Put one stake (possibly sandbags) near the edge of the hole to rest the stock of your rifle on. Then put another stake forward of the rear (first) stake/sandbag toward each dangerous approach. The forward stakes are used to hold the rifle barrel.

E. Emplace grazing fire logs or sandbags to achieve grazing fire 1 meter above ground level.

F. Decide whether to build OHC up or down, based on potential undead observation of position.

G. Scoop out elbow holes to keep your elbows from moving around when you fire.

H. Trace position outline.

I. Clear primary and secondary fields of fire.

Note: *Keep in mind that the widths of all the fighting positions are only an approximate distance. This is due to the individual soldier's equipment such as the Interceptor Body Armor and the modular lightweight load-carrying equipment.*

➤ *Prone position (hasty)*

Stage 2

3.12. Place supports for OHC stringers and construct parapet retaining walls:

A. Emplace OHC supports to front and rear of position.

B. Ensure you have at least 12 inches (30 centimeters), which is about a one-helmet-length distance from the edge of the hole to the beginning of the supports needed for the OHC.

C. If you plan to use logs or cut timber, secure them in place with strong stakes from 2 to 3 inches (5 to 7 centimeters) in diameter and 18 inches (46 centimeters) long. Short, U-shaped pickets will work.

D. Dig in about half the height.

   a. Front retaining wall—at least 10 inches (25 centimeters) high, two filled sandbags deep, and two M16s long.

   b. Rear retaining wall—at least 10 inches (25 centimeters) high and one M16 long.

   c. Flank retaining walls—at least 10 inches (25 centimeters) high and one M16 long.

Stage 3

3.13. Dig position and place stringers for OHC.

A. Ensure maximum depth is armpit deep (if soil conditions permit).

B. Use spoil from hole to fill parapets in the order of front, flanks, and rear.

C. Dig walls vertically.

D. If site soil properties cause unstable soil conditions, construct revetments and consider sloping walls.

E. For sloped walls first dig a vertical hole and then slope walls at a 1:4 ratio (move 12 inches [30 centimeters] horizontally for each 4 feet [1.22 meters] vertically).

F. Dig two grenade sumps in the floor (one on each end). If a member of the undead throws a grenade into the hole, kick or throw it into one of the sumps. The sump will absorb most of the blast. The rest of the blast will be directed straight up and out of the hole. Dig the grenade sumps as wide as the entrenching tool blade, at least as deep as an entrenching tool, and as long as the position floor is wide.

Note: A commonly asked question is: Do zombies have grenades? The answer is that while the undead lack sophisticated weaponry, they can lob a grenade back toward where it came. Unlike a human soldier, a zombie has no fear and in fact is drawn to the metal and smoke. While some will meet their end this way, a few will return grenade fire, so it is better to be safe than sorry.

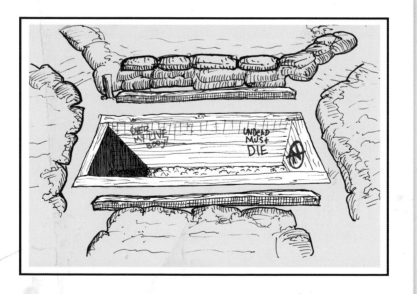

➤ *Two-man fighting position (stage 3)*

G. Dig a storage compartment in the bottom of the back wall; the size of the compartment depends on the amount of equipment and ammunition to be stored.

Install revetments to prevent wall collapse/cave-in:

a. Required in unstable soil conditions.

b. Use plywood or sheeting material and pickets to revet walls.

c. Tie back pickets and posts.

d. Emplace OHC stringers.

e. Use two-by-fours, four-by-fours, or pickets ("U" facing down).

f. Make OHC stringers standard length, which is 8 feet (2.4 meters). This is long enough to allow sufficient length in case walls slope.

g. Use "L" for stringer length and "H" for stringer spacing.

H. Remove the second layer of sandbags in the front and rear retaining walls to make room for the stringers. Place the same sandbags on top of the stringers once you have the stringers properly positioned.

Stage 4

3.14. Install OHC and camouflage:

A. Install overhead cover.

B. Use plywood, sheeting mats as a dustproof layer (could be boxes, plastic panel, or interlocked U-shaped pickets). Standard dustproof layer is 4-by-4-foot sheets of 3/4-inch plywood centered over dug position.

C. Nail plywood dustproof layer to stringers.

D. Use at least 18 inches (46 centimeters) of sand-filled sandbags for overhead burst protection (four layers). At a minimum these sandbags must cover an area that extends to the sandbags used for the front and rear retaining walls.

E. Use plastic or a poncho for waterproofing layer.

F. Fill center cavity with soil from dug hold and surrounding soil.

G. Use surrounding topsoil and camouflage screen systems.

H. Use soil from hole to fill sandbags, OHC cavity, and blend in with surroundings.

Note: *While you are doing the unpleasant work of securing your shelter, know that the undead make no such preparations. Other than open graves and loose caskets, zombies have no shelters and thus exist with the rot, insects, and infection. Here the living have an advantage.*

➤ *Machine gun fighting position with OHC*

The Fear of Zombies

There's no better insight into a soldier's frame of mind than the places where he lives, sleeps, and works. Such is the case with the shelters and fighting positions created by our nation's fighting men in the early days of their battles against the Gray Menace. These two examples of entrenched fighting positions reflect the enormous, almost paranoid fear with which the average G.I. Joe considered zombies in those early days. Note the heavy armament, the desperately aggressive graffiti—is it any surprise to learn that soldiers were terrified of encountering zombie forces and fanatically afraid of being bitten?

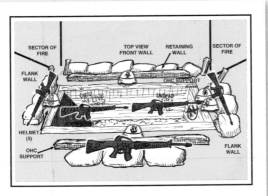

➤ That's quite a lot of firepower for such a small entrenchment!

➤ Note how much like a grave this entrenchment seems, and must have seemed to soldiers of that era.

The Zombie-Fighter's Workplace

Welcome to the soldier's office, the place where he was likely to spend most of his time in the event of a zombie uprising: 6 feet underground, coated in sweat and grease from his machine gun as he fired from a turret of sandbags at the unceasing waves of zombies lumbering slowly but surely in his direction.

What's remarkable about these "workplaces" is how similar they are to the trenches and machine-gun nests used in more traditional warfare. While the Army receives well-deserved praise for its adaptability, the fact is that much of its approach to the zombie menace was to roll out the same concepts as before, only slowly modifying them to fit this extraordinary enemy.

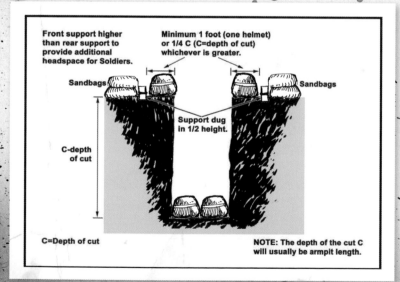

Front support higher than rear support to provide additional headspace for Soldiers.

Minimum 1 foot (one helmet) or 1/4 C (C=depth of cut) whichever is greater.

Sandbags

Sandbags

Support dug in 1/2 height.

C-depth of cut

C=Depth of cut

NOTE: The depth of the cut C will usually be armpit length.

A side view of the zombie-fighting pit gives a sense of how deep these entrenchments went.

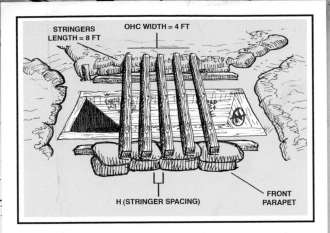

STRINGERS
LENGTH = 8 FT

OHC WIDTH = 4 FT

H (STRINGER SPACING)

FRONT
PARAPET

➤ The use of "stringers" to add camouflage is a prime example of the Army's using outdated techniques: twigs and bushes could do little to disguise the smell of brains, delicious brains from rampaging zombies.

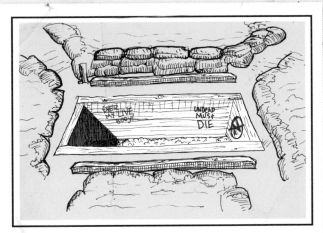

➤ It really looks an awful lot like a grave, doesn't it? Am I just reading too much into this? What do you think that was all about?

OVER MY DEAD BODY

UNDEAD MUST DIE

➤ The soldier clocks in and gets to work.

CLOSE COMBAT MISSILE FIGHTING POSITIONS

3.15. The following paragraphs discuss close combat missile fighting positions for the AT4 and Javelin.

AT4 Position

3.16. The AT4 is fired from the fighting positions previously described. However, backblast may cause friendly casualties of soldiers in the position's backblast area. You should ensure that any walls, parapets, large trees, or other objects to the rear will not deflect the backblast. When the AT4 is fired from a two-soldier position, you must ensure that the backblast area is clear. The front edge of a fighting position is a good elbow rest to help you steady the weapon and gain accuracy. Stability is better if your body is leaning against the position's front or side wall.

Standard Javelin Fighting Position with Overhead Cover

3.17. The standard Javelin fighting position has cover to protect you from direct and indirect fires. The position is prepared in the same way as the two-man fighting position, with two additional steps. First, the back wall of the position is extended and sloped rearward, which serves as storage area. Second, the front and side parapets are extended twice the length as the dimensions of the two-man fighting position with the javelin's primary and secondary seated firing platforms added to both sides.

Note: When a Javelin is fired, the muzzle end extends 6 inches (15 centimeters) beyond the front of the position, and the rear launcher extends out over the rear of the position. As the missile leaves the launcher, stabilizing fins unfold. You must keep the weapon at least 6 inches (15 centimeters) above the ground when firing to leave room for the fins. OHC that would allow firing from beneath it is usually built if the backblast area is clear.

CHAPTER 4

MOVEMENT

At the core of the Army's shift from a zombie-killing to a zombie-rehabilitating force was a change in the military's understanding of what the zombie was, and what motivated him.

For that reason, this chapter's penetrating psychological insight into what makes the dead keep walking is of great historical interest. For as long as the Army believed that the dead walked *just because*, or with a single-minded fixation on brains, it was destined to see the Gray Menace as a terrifying foe, the stuff of nightmares.

—Historian's note

Movement

Since the undead are always advancing and never retreating, you will spend more time moving than fighting. The fundamentals of movement discussed in this chapter provide techniques that all soldiers must learn. Even seasoned troops should practice these techniques regularly until they become second nature.

Movement Techniques

Movement in urban areas is the first skill you must master. Movement techniques must be practiced until they become second nature. To reduce exposure to undead bombardment, you should avoid open areas, avoid silhouetting yourself, and select your next covered position before movement. The following paragraphs discuss how to move in urban areas.

Avoiding Open Areas

4.1. Open areas, such as streets, alleys, and parks, should be avoided. They are natural kill zones for the undead. They can be crossed safely if the individual applies certain fundamentals, including using smoke from hand grenades or smoke pots to conceal movement. When smoke has been thrown in an open area, the undead may choose to engage by charging into the smoke cloud.

Note: *The undead are less likely to charge if the smoke is not brightly colored.*

Moving Parallel to Buildings

4.2. You may not always be able to use the inside of buildings as routes of advance and must move on the outside of the buildings. Smoke, suppressive fires, and cover and concealment should be used as much as possible to hide movement. You should move parallel to the side of the building, maintaining at least 12 inches of separation between yourself and the wall to avoid reach-arounds or reach-throughs (the undead reaching around corners or through openings in the wall). Stay in the shadows, present a low silhouette, and move rapidly to your next position. If a zombie inside the building reveals itself, it exposes itself to fire from other squad members providing overwatch.

Moving Past Windows

4.3. Windows present another hazard to the soldier. The most common mistakes are exposing the head in a first-floor window and not being aware of basement windows—a favorite ambush spot for the undead. When using the correct technique for passing a first-floor window, you must stay below the window level and near the side of the building. Ensure you do not silhouette yourself in the window. An undead assailant inside the building would have to expose itself to covering fires if it tries to engage you.

➤ *Soldier moving past windows*

4.4. The same techniques used in passing first-floor windows are used when passing basement windows. You should not walk or run past a basement window, as this will present a good target for an undead assailant inside the building. Ensure that you stay close to the wall of

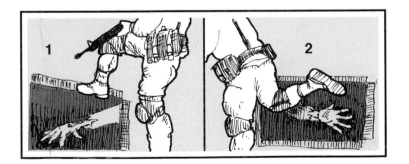

➤ *Soldier passing basement windows*

the building and step or jump past the window without exposing your legs.

Crossing a Wall

4.5. You must learn the correct method of crossing a wall. After you have reconnoitered the other side, quickly roll over the wall and keep a low silhouette. Your speed of movement and low silhouette deny the undead a good target.

Moving around Corners

4.6. The area around a corner must be observed before the soldier moves. The most common mistake you can make at a corner is allowing your weapon to extend beyond the corner, exposing your position; this mistake is known as *flagging* your weapon. You should show your head below the height where a zombie would expect to see it. You must lie

> *Correct technique for looking around a corner*

flat on the ground and not extend your weapon beyond the corner of the building. Only expose your head (at ground level) enough to permit observation. You can also use a mirror, if available, to look around the corner. Another corner-clearing technique that is used when speed is required is the *pie-ing* method. This procedure is done by aiming the weapon beyond the corner into the direction of travel (without flagging) and sidestepping around the corner in a circular fashion with the muzzle as the pivot point.

Moving within a Building

4.7. Once you have entered a building, follow these procedures to move around in it:

Doors and Windows

4.8. Avoid silhouetting yourself in doors and windows.

Hallways

4.9. When moving in hallways, never move alone—always move with at least one other soldier for security.

Walls

4.10. You should try to stay 12 to 18 inches away from walls when moving. Rubbing against walls may alert a zombie on the other side; or, if you are engaged by a zombie, you can be pinned to a wall.

Fighting Positions

How do you find and use a fighting position properly? You have to know this: Whether you are attacking or defending, your success depends on your ability to place accurate fire on the undead—with the least exposure to return attack.

Hasty Fighting Position

4.11. A hasty fighting position is normally occupied in the attack or early stages of defense. It is a position from which you can place fire upon the undead while using available cover for protection from return attack. You may occupy it voluntarily or be forced to occupy it due to undead lunging at you. In either case the position lacks preparation before occupation. Some of the more common hasty fighting positions in an urban area are corners of buildings, behind walls, windows, unprepared loopholes, and peaks of roofs.

➤ *Soldiers in fighting positions*

Corners of Buildings

4.12. You must be able to fire your weapon (both right- and left-handed) to be effective around corners.

A common error made in firing around corners is firing from the wrong shoulder. This exposes more of your body to return attack than necessary. By firing from the proper shoulder, you can reduce exposure to undead bombardment.

Note: *Remember that the undead may be lurking around every corner. Do not blindly reach around and fire your weapon. A zombie could bite you or end up being at point-blank range, and when shot, it could explode, spraying infected blood everywhere and contaminating the area. Another common mistake when firing around corners is firing from the standing position. If the soldier exposes himself at the height the undead expects, then he risks exposing the entire length of his body as a target for the undead.*

➤ *Soldier firing around a corner*

Windows

4.13. In an urban area windows provide convenient firing ports. Avoid firing from the standing position, which exposes most of your body to attack from the undead and which could silhouette you against a light-colored interior background. This is an obvious sign of your position, especially at night, when the muzzle flash can be easily observed. To fire from a window properly, remain well back in the room to hide the flash and kneel to limit exposure and avoid silhouetting yourself.

4.14. You may fire through a hole created in the wall and avoid windows. You must stay well back from the loophole so the muzzle of the weapon does not protrude beyond the wall and the muzzle flash is concealed.

Roof

4.15. The peak of a roof provides a vantage point that increases field of vision and the ranges at which you can engage targets. A chimney, smokestack, or any other object protruding from the roof of a building should be used to reduce the size of the target exposed.

➤ *Soldier firing from the peak of a roof*

Prepared Fighting Position

4.16. A prepared firing position is one built or improved to allow you to engage a particular area, avenue of approach, or undead position, while reducing your exposure to return attack. Examples of prepared positions include barricaded windows; fortified loopholes; and sniper, antiarmor, and machine-gun positions.

Barricaded Window

4.17. The natural firing port provided by windows can be improved by barricading the window, leaving a small hole for you to use. Materials torn from the interior walls of the building or any other available material may be used for barricading.

4.18. Barricade all windows, whether you intend to use them as firing ports or not. Keep the undead guessing. Avoid making neat, square, or rectangular holes, which clearly identify your firing positions to the undead. For example, a barricaded window should not have a neat, regular firing port. The window should remain in its original condition so that your position is hard to detect. Firing from the bottom of the window gives you the advantage of the wall because the firing port is less obvious to the undead. Sandbags are used to reinforce the wall below the window and to increase protection. All glass must be removed from the window to prevent injury. Lace curtains permit you to see out and prevent the undead from seeing in. Wire mesh over the window keeps the undead from throwing in hand grenades.

Protection

Two layers of sandbags are placed on the floor to protect you from undead reach-throughs from a lower floor (if the position is on the second floor or higher). Construct a wall of sandbags, rubble, and furniture to the rear of the position as protection from the undead in the room. A table, bedstead, or other available material can provide OHC (overhead cover) for the position.

Camouflage

Hide the position in plain sight by knocking other holes in the wall, making it difficult for the undead to determine which hole the fire is coming from. Remove exterior siding in several places to make loopholes less noticeable.

Backblast

Shoulder-launched missile (SLM) and close combat missile (CCM) crews may be hampered in choosing firing positions due to the backblast of their weapons. They may not have enough time to knock out walls in buildings and clear backblast areas. They should select positions that allow the backblast to escape, such as corner windows where the round fired goes out one window and the backblast escapes from another.

SLMs and CCMs

Various principles of employing SLM and CCM weapons have universal applications. These include using available cover, providing mutual support, and allowing for backblast. However, urban areas require additional considerations. Soldiers must select numerous alternate positions and position their weapons in the shadows and within the building.

A gunner firing an AT4 or Javelin from the top of a building can use a chimney for cover, if available. When selecting firing positions for his SLM or CCM, a soldier uses rubble, corners of buildings, or destroyed vehicles as cover. He moves his weapon along rooftops to find better

Danger

When firing within an enclosure, ensure that it measures at least 10 feet by 15 feet (150 square feet); is clear of debris and other loose objects; and has windows, doors, or holes in the walls where the backblast can escape.

➤ *Emplacement of machine gun in a doorway*

angles. On tall buildings he can use the building itself as overhead cover. He must select a position where backblast will not damage or collapse the building or injure him.

Gun Positions

The machine gunner can emplace his weapon almost anywhere. In the attack, windows and doors offer ready-made firing ports. For this reason, avoid windows and doors, which the undead normally have under observation. Use any opening created in walls during the fighting. Small explosive charges can create loopholes for machine-gun positions. Ensure that machine guns are inside the building and that they remain in the shadows.

Upon occupying a building, board up all windows and doors. Leave small gaps between the boards for use as alternate positions.

Loopholes

Use loopholes extensively in the defense. Avoid constructing them in any logical pattern, or all at floor or tabletop levels. Varying height and location makes them hard to pinpoint and identify. Make dummy loopholes and knock off shingles to aid in the deception. Construct loopholes behind shrubbery, under doorjambs, and under the eaves of buildings, because these are hard to detect.

You can increase your fields of fire by locating the machine gun in the corner of the building or in the cellar. To add cover and concealment, integrate available materials, such as desks, overstuffed chairs, couches, and other items of furniture, into the construction of bunkers.

Grazing fire is ideal but sometimes impractical or impossible. Where destroyed vehicles, rubble, and other obstructions restrict the fields of grazing fire, elevate the gun to allow you to fire over obstacles. You might have to fire from second- or third-story loopholes.

CHAPTER 5

COMBAT MARKSMANSHIP

Of all the chapters in the volume you see before you, there is perhaps none that will bring a tear to the eye of a grizzled old zombie-fighter more quickly or more surely than this one. After all, "Combat Marksmanship" is a literal master class in taking down the Gray Menace: Aiming for the skull, "poppin' brains," and holding fire until you see the yellow of their eyes all are emphasized in this chapter.

Imagine the unease and disappointment when veterans of the old brain-splattering days regard today's fighting forces, where the emphasis is on taking Military Working Zombies "alive"—that is, as alive as they're liable to get at this point. As a point of historical interest, most will find this chapter, with its armory of zombie-felling weaponry, quite fascinating. Old zombie-hunters, however, may wish to skip ahead to the next chapter.

—Historian's note

Caliber	....	126 mm
Weight (missile+CLU)	....	49.5 lb
Maximum effective range	....	2,000 meters (direct and top-attack)
Minimum effective engagement range		
Direct attack	....	65 meters
Top attack	....	150 meters
Minimum enclosure		
Length	....	15 feet
Width	....	12 feet
Height	....	7 feet

Combat Marksmanship

Combat marksmanship is essential to all soldiers—not only to acquire the expert skills necessary for survival on the battlefield but because it enforces teamwork and discipline. In every organization all members must continue to practice certain skills to remain proficient. Marksmanship is paramount.

This chapter discusses several aspects of combat marksmanship, including safety, administrative issues, and weapons.

WEAPONS

5.1. Weapons include the M9 pistol; M16-series rifles; M4 carbine rifles; M203 grenade launcher; M249 squad automatic weapon (SAW); M240B machine gun; M2 .50-caliber machine gun; MK 19 grenade machine gun, Mod 3; improved M72 light anti-undead weapon; M136 AT4; M141 bunker (and death)-defeating munition; and Javelin shoulder-fired munition.

M9 Pistol

5.2. A lightweight, semiautomatic, single-action/double-action pistol can be unloaded without activating the trigger while the safety is in the "on" position. The M9 has a 15-round staggered magazine. The reversible magazine release button can be positioned for either right- or left-handed shooters. This gun may be fired without a magazine inserted. The M9 is only authorized for 9-mm ball or dummy ammunition manufactured to U.S. and NATO specifications. On this weapon the hammer may be lowered from the cocked, ready-to-fire position to the uncocked

Caliber	9 mm
Weight	
Unloaded	2.1 lb
Fully loaded	2.6 lb
Maximum effective range	50 meters

➤ *M9 pistol*

position without activating the trigger. This is done by placing the thumb safety "on."

Note: While most living enemies will respond when confronted with a soldier's unlocking of a safety or the cocking of a hammer, a zombie will not.

M16-Series Rifles

5.3. A lightweight, air-cooled, gas-operated, magazine-fed rifle designed for either burst or semiautomatic fire through use of a selector lever. There are three models.

M16A2

5.4. The M16A2 incorporates improvements in iron sight, pistol grip, stock, and overall combat effectiveness. Accuracy is enhanced by an improved muzzle compensator, a three-round burst control, and a heavier barrel; and by using the heavier NATO-standard ammunition, which is also fired by the squad automatic weapon (SAW).

M16A3

5.5. The M16A3 is identical to the M16A2 except that it has a removable carrying handle mounted on a Picatinny rail (for better mounting of optics).

M16A4

5.6. The M16A4 is identical to the M16A2 except for the removable carrying handle mounted on a Picatinny rail. It has a maximum effective range of 600 meters for area targets. Like the M4-series weapons, the M16-series rifles use ball, tracer, dummy, blank, and short-range training ammunition manufactured to U.S. and NATO specifications.

M4 Carbine

5.7. The M4 is a compact version of the M16A2 rifle, with collapsible stock, flat-top upper receiver accessory rail, and detachable handle/rear aperture site assembly. This rifle enables a soldier operating in close quarters to engage targets at extended ranges with accurate, lethal fire.

M203 Grenade Launcher

5.8. The M203A1 grenade launcher is a single-shot weapon designed for use with the M4 series carbine. It fires a 40-mm grenade. Both have a leaf sight and quadrant sight. The M203 fires high-explosive, high-explosive dual-purpose round, buckshot, illumination, signal, CS (riot control), and training practice (TP) ammunition.

Caliber..40 mm

Weight..3.0 lb (empty)
3.6 lb (loaded)

Maximum effective range

Area target..350 meters
Point target ....150 meters

Rate of fire ....5 to 7 rounds per minute

➤ *M203 grenade launcher*

M249 SAW

5.9. A lightweight, gas-operated, air-cooled, belt- or magazine-fed, one-man-portable automatic weapon that fires from the open-bolt position. This gun can be fired from the shoulder, hip, or underarm position; from the bipod-steadied position; or from the tripod-mounted position. Two M249s are issued per Infantry squad.

Caliber	5.56 mm
Weight	16.5 lb

Maximum effective range

Area target	Tripod	1,000 m
	Bipod	800 m
Point target	Tripod	800 m
	Bipod	600 m

Rate of fire

Sustained	100 rounds per min
	6- to 9-round bursts
	4 to 5 seconds between bursts
	Barrel change every 10 minutes
Rapid	200 rounds per minute
	6- to 9-round bursts
	2 to 3 seconds between bursts
	Barrel change every 2 minutes
Cyclic	650 to 850 rounds per minute
	Continuous burst
	Barrel change every minute

➤ *M249 SAW*

M240B Machine Gun

5.10. A medium, belt-fed, air-cooled, gas-operated, crew-served, fully automatic weapon that fires from the open-bolt position. Ammunition is fed into the weapon from a 100-round bandolier containing ball and tracer (4:1 mix) ammunition with disintegrating metallic split-link belt. Other types of ammunition available include armor-piercing, blank, and dummy rounds. It can be mounted on a bipod, tripod, aircraft, or vehicle. A spare barrel is issued with each M240B, and barrels can be changed quickly as the weapon has a fixed headspace.

M2 .50 Caliber Machine Gun

5.11. A heavy (barrel), recoil-operated, air-cooled, crew-served, and transportable fully automatic weapon with adjustable headspace. A disintegrating metallic link belt is used to feed the ammunition into the weapon. This gun may be mounted on ground mounts and most vehicles as an anti–aircraft/light armor weapon.

MK 19 Grenade Machine Gun, Mod 3

5.12. A self-powered, air-cooled, belt-fed, blowback-operated weapon designed to deliver decisive firepower against the undead. A disintegrating metallic link belt feeds either high-explosive or high-explosive dual-purpose ammunition through the left side of the weapon. It is the main suppressive weapon for combat support and combat service support units.

Caliber	40 mm
Weight	72.5 lb

Maximum effective range

Area target	2,212 meters
Point target	1,500 meters

Rate of fire

Sustained	40 rounds per minute
Rapid	60 rounds per minute
Cyclic	325 to 375 rounds per minute

➤ *MK 19 grenade machine gun*

Improved M72 Light Anti-Undead Weapon

5.13. A compact, lightweight, single-shot, and disposable weapon with a family of warheads originally designed to defeat lightly armored vehicles and other hard targets at close-combat ranges. Issued as a round of ammunition, it requires no maintenance. The improved M72 light anti-undead weapon systems offer significantly enhanced capability beyond that of the combat-proven M72A3. The improved M72 light anti-undead weapon system consists of an unguided high-explosive rocket prepackaged in a telescoping, throwaway launcher.

Note: *Seldom do zombies use armor, though in battle some semi-intelligent zombies have sheltered themselves from mortar with sheet metal or plywood. The undead enemy often congregates in large hordes, making the M72 effective for large kills. The semi-intelligent undead have also on occasion* operated vehicles short distances, sometimes enabling them to enter the fortified doors of farmhouses, hospitals, and laboratories. In such cases anti-armor weapons are especially useful in the battle against the undead.

M136 AT4

5.14. The M136 AT4 is a lightweight, self-contained pro-living weapon. It is man-portable and fires (only) from the right shoulder. The M136 AT4 is used primarily by Infantry forces to engage and defeat large hording undead threats. The weapon accurately delivers a high-explosive anti-death warhead with excellent penetration capability (more than 15 feet of solid undead bodies) and lethal after-penetration effects.

M141 Bunker (and Death)-Defeating Munition

5.15. A lightweight, self-contained, man-portable, high-explosive, dis-posable, shoulder-launched, multipurpose assault weapon-disposable that contains all gunner features and controls necessary to aim, fire, and engage targets.

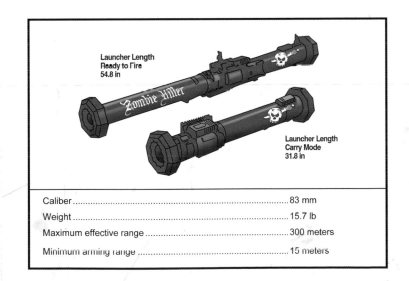

Launcher Length
Ready to Fire
54.8 in

Launcher Length
Carry Mode
31.8 in

Caliber	83 mm
Weight	15.7 lb
Maximum effective range	300 meters
Minimum arming range	15 meters

➤ M141 BDM

Javelin

5.16. The Javelin is the first *fire-and-forget*, crew-served anti-death missile. Its F&F guidance mode enables gunners to fire and then immediately take cover. This greatly increases survivability. The Javelin's two major components are a reusable command launch unit and a missile sealed in a disposable launch tube assembly. Special features include a selectable top-attack or direct-fire mode (for targets under cover or for use in urban terrain against bunkers and buildings), target lock-on before launch, and a very limited backblast.

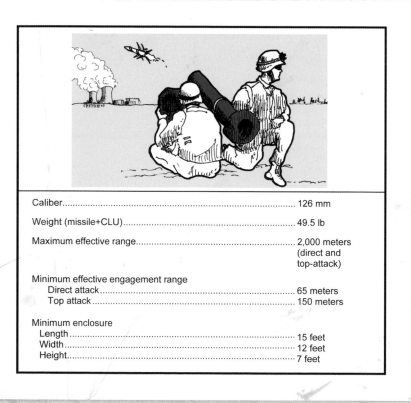

Caliber	126 mm
Weight (missile+CLU)	49.5 lb
Maximum effective range	2,000 meters (direct and top-attack)
Minimum effective engagement range	
Direct attack	65 meters
Top attack	150 meters
Minimum enclosure	
Length	15 feet
Width	12 feet
Height	7 feet

➤*Javelin*

FIRE CONTROL

5.17. Fire control includes all actions in planning, preparing, and applying fire on a target. Your leader selects and designates targets. He also designates the midpoint and flanks or ends of a target, unless they are obvious for you to identify.

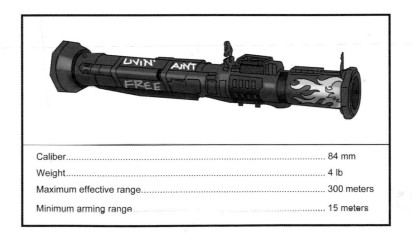

Caliber .... 66 mm

Weight .... 2.2 lb

Maximum effective range .... 220 meters

Minimum arming range .... 10 meters

➤ *Improved M72 light anti-undead weapon*

Caliber.. 84 mm

Weight.. 4 lb

Maximum effective range.. 300 meters

Minimum arming range.. 15 meters

➤ *M136 AT4*

Threat-Based Fire Control Measures

5.18. The following paragraphs discuss threat-based fire control measures.

Engagement Priorities

5.19. Engagement priorities are the target types, identified by your leader, that offer the greatest payoff or present the greatest threat. He then establishes these as a unit engagement priority.

Range Selection

5.20. Range selection is a means by which your leader will use his estimate of the situation to specify the range and ammunition for the engagement. Range selection is dependent on the anticipated engagement range. Terrain, visibility, weather, and light conditions affect range selection, and the amount and type of ammunition.

Weapons Control Status

5.21. The three levels of weapons control status outline the conditions, based on target identification criteria, under which friendly elements may engage. The three levels, in descending order of restriction, follow:

A. Weapons Hold: Engage only if charged by the undead or ordered to engage.

B. Weapons Tight: Only engage targets that are positively identified as undead.

C. Weapons Free: Engage any targets that are not positively identified as friendly.

> *Advanced zombie-fighting technology*

REFLEXIVE FIRE

5.22. Reflexive fire is the automatic trained response to fire your weapon with minimal reaction time. Reflexive shooting allows little or no margin for error. Once you master these fundamentals, they will be your key to survival on the battlefield:

- Proper firing stance.

- Proper weapon-ready position.

- Aim point.

Proper Firing Stance

5.23. Regardless of the ready position used, always assume the correct firing stance to ensure proper stability and accuracy when engaging targets. Remember that zombies, while extremely slow, do tend to sway and lunge and stumble and therefore can at times make difficult targets. Every soldier thus must have a solid stance in battle. Keep your feet about shoulder-width apart. Toes are pointed straight to the front (direction of movement). The firing side foot is slightly staggered to the rear of the nonfiring side foot. Knees are slightly bent and the upper body is leaned slightly forward. Shoulders are square and pulled back, not rolled over or slouched. Keep your head up and both eyes open. When engaging targets, hold the weapon with the butt of the weapon firmly against your shoulder and the firing side elbow close against the body.

High-Ready Position

Hold the butt of the weapon under your armpit, with the barrel pointed slightly up so that the top of the front sight post is just below your line of sight but within your peripheral vision. With your nonfiring hand grasp the handguards toward the front sling swivel. Place your trigger finger outside the trigger well and the thumb of your firing hand on the selector lever. To engage a target from this position, just push the weapon forward as if to bayonet the target and bring the butt stock firmly against your shoulder as it slides up your body. This technique is best suited for the lineup outside of a building, room, or bunker entrance.

Note: Remember that no matter your aiming technique, taking down a zombie does not necessarily mean you have eliminated him. They will keep coming regardless of lost arms, legs, even heads. Watch them carefully after they're down. If they move, reengage.

Aim Point

5.24. Undead engagements fall into two categories.

Lethal Shot Placement

The lethal zone of an undead target is the head. Destruction of the parts of the brain called the cerebellum and/or the brainstem will kill him. Decapitation will also successfully terminate a zombie.

Incapacitating Shot Placement

No shot placement will guarantee immediate and total incapacitation without termination. But a shot roughly centered in the face comes close. Shots to the side of the head should be centered between the crown of the skull and the middle of the ear opening, and from the center of the cheekbones to the middle of the back of the head.

Caliber	.50
Ammunition	12.7 x 99-mm NATO
Weight	84 lb (44 lb for tripod)
Maximum effective range	
Antiaircraft mount	1,400 meters
Tripod mount	2,000 meters
Rate of fire	
Cyclic	400 to 500 rounds per minute

➤ *Superior firepower*

CHAPTER 6

SURVIVAL, EVASION, RESISTANCE, AND ESCAPE

By this chapter you've got a feel for this generation's crop of zombie-fighters. Reading over the chapter that follows, you might imagine a ticker-tape parade awaiting the brave young soldier who shot his way through a pack of zombies, running like hell as their gnarled fingers scraped the uniform right off his back, and managed to outrun the lumbering ghoulies to safety. In the early days it was enough to survive, evade, resist, and escape.

Not so today. A new recruit, fresh out of basic training, who turned tail and ran with a pack of Military Working Zombies in hot pursuit would be as liable as not to spend the next few days in the brig for forfeiting valuable Army assets. Gone are the days when such a soldier would be welcomed back to camp with a hot meal, a warm shower, and a good night's sleep—more likely he'd be scrubbing toilets with a toothbrush if he failed to come back to base with anything less than a whole flock of captured zombies trailing behind him.

—Historian's note

Survival, Evasion, Resistance, and Escape

Continuous operations and fast-moving battles increase your chances of becoming either temporarily separated from your unit or trapped among the undead alone. Whatever the case, your top priority should be rejoining your unit or making it to friendly lines. If you do become isolated, every soldier must continue to fight, evade capture, and regain contact with friendly forces. If captured, detained, or held hostage, individual soldiers must live, act, and speak in a manner that leaves no doubt they adhere to the traditions and values of the U.S. Army and the Code of Conduct.

SURVIVAL

6.1. The acrostic SURVIVAL can help guide your actions in any situation. Learn what each letter represents, and practice applying these guidelines when conducting survival training:

6.2. A useful technique for organizing survival is the three-phase individual survival kit. The content of each phase of the kit depends on the environment in the AO and available supplies. An example of the contents of a three-phase survival kit is as follows:

➤ *Look behind you!*

6.3. Items to be carried (and their suggested uses) include:

- Safety pins in hat (fishhooks or for holding torn clothes together).

- Heavy-duty knife with sharpener, bayonet type (heavy chopping, cutting, or decapitating).

- Mirror (signaling).

- Tape (utility work).

- Aspirin.

- Clear plastic bag (water purification, solar stills).

- Candles (heat, light).

- Surgical tubing (snares, weapons, drinking tube).

- Tripwire (traps, snares, weapons).

- Dental floss (cordage, fishing line, tie-down, traps).

- Upholstery needles (sewing, fishhooks).

EVASION

6.4. Evasion is the action you take to stay out of the undead's hands when separated from your unit and in zombie territory. There are several courses of action you can take to avoid being devoured and rejoin your unit. You may stay in your current position and wait for friendly troops to find you, or you may try to move and find friendly lines. Below are a few guidelines you can follow.

Planning

6.5. Planning is essential to achieve successful evasion. Follow these guidelines for successful evasion:

- Keep a positive attitude.

- Use established procedures.

- Follow your EPA (evasion plan of action).

- Be patient.

- Drink water.

- Conserve strength for critical periods.

- Rest and sleep as much as possible.

- Stay out of sight.

Odors

6.6. Avoid the following odors (they stand out and may give you away):

- Florally scented soaps and shampoos.

- Shaving cream, after-shave lotion, or other cosmetics.

- Insect repellent (camouflage stick is least scented).

- Gum and candy (smell is strong or sweet).

- Tobacco (odor is unmistakable).

Note: *Mask scent using crushed grasses, dead animals, berries, dirt, and charcoal.*

Evasion Plan of Action

6.7. Establish:

- Suitable area for recovery.

- Selected area for evasion.

> *Natural cover*

- Neutral or friendly country or area.

- Designated area for recovery.

Choose hiding places that are least likely to be mobbed by the undead, for example, antiques shops, New Wave churches, discos in urban areas, caves in high elevations, hideouts near fast-flowing bodies of water, and treetops in rural areas. Avoid cemeteries and lone farmhouses at all costs.

Movement

6.8. Remember, a moving object is easy to spot. If travel is necessary:

- Mask with natural cover.

- Restrict to periods of bright sunshine, lovely weather, wind, or reduced undead activity.

- Avoid silhouetting.

- *Do* the following at irregular intervals:
  - —*Stop* at a point of concealment.
  - —*Look* for signs of living human or animal activity (such as smoke, tracks, roads, troops, vehicles, aircraft, wire, and buildings). Watch for open graves or sleeping undead (you do NOT want to step on a sleeping zombie), and avoid leaving evidence of travel. Peripheral vision is more effective for recognizing movement at night and twilight.
  - —*Listen* for vehicles, troops, aircraft, weapons, animals, and so forth.
  - —*Smell* for vehicles, troops, animals, fires, the rotting flesh of the undead, and so forth.

- Camouflage evidence of travel. Route selection requires detailed planning and special techniques (irregular route/zigzag).

- Conceal evidence of travel, using techniques such as:
  - —Avoid disturbing vegetation.
  - —Do not break branches, leaves, or grass. Use a walking stick to part vegetation and push it back to its original position.
  - —Do not grab small trees or brush. (This may scuff the bark or create movement that is easily spotted. In snow country this creates a path of snow-less vegetation, revealing your route.)
  - —Pick firm footing (carefully place the foot lightly but squarely on the surface to avoid slipping).
  - —Avoid the loose or overturned ground commonly found in zombie-populated areas, such as upturned burial sites.

- Try not to:
  - —Overturn ground cover, rocks, and sticks.
  - —Scuff bark on logs and sticks.
  - —Make noise by breaking sticks. (Cloth wrapped around feet helps muffle noise.)

—Mangle grass and bushes that normally spring back.

- Mask unavoidable tracks in soft footing.
  —Place tracks in the shadows of vegetation, downed logs, and snowdrifts.
  —Move before and during precipitation, which allows tracks to fill in.
  —Travel during windy periods.
  —Take advantage of solid surfaces (such as logs and rocks), leaving less evidence of travel.
  —Tie cloth or vegetation to feet, or pat out tracks lightly to speed their breakdown or make them look old.

- While it is uncommon, on occasion the semi-intelligent undead have utilized undead dogs (aka Hounds of Hell) against the living. Cited by some as mere urban myths, these canines—as depicted in such pop films as *I Am Legend*—do, in fact, pose a threat. If pursued by the HoH, concentrate on defeating the handler.

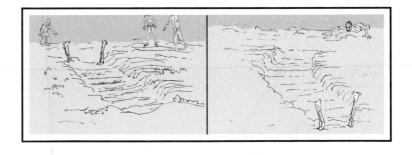

➤*An example of the zombie's skill at hiding*

Rules for Escaping a Zombie Hellhound Incursion

- Travel downwind of dog/handler, if possible.

- Travel over rough terrain and/or through dense vegetation to slow the handler.

- Travel downstream through fast-moving water.

- Zigzag route if possible, consider loop-backs and "J" hooks.

- Penetrate obstacles as follows:

    —Enter deep ditches feet first to avoid injury.

    —Go around chain-link and wire fences. Go under fence if unavoidable, crossing at damaged areas. *Do not* touch fence; look for electrical insulators or security devices.

    —Penetrate rail fences, passing under or between lower rails. If this is impractical, go over the top, presenting as low a silhouette as possible.

    —Cross roads after observation from concealment to determine undead activity. Cross at points offering concealment such as bushes, shadows, or bends in the road. Cross in a manner leaving footprints parallel (cross step sideways) to the road.

RESISTANCE

Article I

Soldiers have a duty to support living interests and oppose the living's enemies regardless of the circumstances, whether located in a combat environment or OOTW (operations other than war) resulting in entrapment by the undead. Past experience of captured living soldiers reveals that honorable survival during entrapment requires that the soldier possess a high degree of dedication and motivation. Maintaining these qualities requires knowledge of, and a strong belief in, the following:

- The advantages of living institutions and concepts.

Code of Conduct

I.   I am living, fighting in the forces which guard my country, my earth, and our way of life. I am prepared to give my life in their defense.

II.   I will never surrender of my own free will. If in command, I will never surrender the members of my command while they still have the means to resist.

III.   If I am entrapped, I will continue to resist by all means available, I will make every effort to escape and aid others to escape. I will accept neither parole nor special favors from the undead.

IV.   If I become a prisoner of war, I will keep faith with my fellow prisoners and terminate them should they become undead or sympathetic. I will give no information or take part in any action which might be harmful to my comrades. If I am senior, I will take command. If not, I will obey the lawful orders of those appointed over me and will back them up in every way.

V.   When questioned by a semi-intelligent zombie should I become a prisoner of war, I am required to give only name, rank, service number, and date of birth. I will evade answering further questions to the utmost of my ability.

VI.   I will never forget that I am a member of the living, fighting for freedom and life, responsible for my actions, and dedicated to the principles that keep my country and earth alive. I will trust in my God and in the living United States of America and earth.

- Love and faith in the living and a conviction that the living cause is just.

- Faith and loyalty to fellow entrapped soldiers.

Article II

Members of the Armed Forces may never surrender voluntarily. Even when isolated and no longer able to inflict casualties on the undead or otherwise defend themselves, soldiers must try to evade entrapment and rejoin the nearest friendly force. Surrender is the willful act of members of the Armed Forces turning themselves over to undead forces to be devoured and/or turned into zombies. Surrender is always dishonorable and never allowed. When there is no chance for meaningful resistance, evasion is impossible, and further fighting would lead to death with no significant loss to the undead, members of Armed Forces should view themselves as "captured" against their will, versus a circumstance that is seen as voluntarily "surrendering." Soldiers must remember the capture was dictated by the futility of the situation and overwhelming undead strengths.

Article III

The misfortune of capture does not lessen the duty of a member of the Armed Forces to continue resisting undead exploitation and zombie-fication by all means available. Contrary to the Transylvania Conventions, undead enemies whom living forces have engaged since 1949 have regarded the captured soldier as nothing more than a vessel for brains. In the past, undead enemies of the living have immediately begun devouring soldiers upon their capture. Soldiers have been bitten, scratched, pinched, bled on, suppurated on, defecated on, and drooled upon. Nevertheless, captured soldiers must take advantage of escape opportunities and make every attempt to avoid contact with zombies that would cause infection and zombie-fication. If the fortunate case occurs in which you are approached by a semi-intelligent zombie, do not sign or enter into any parole agreement. Just be glad the zombie is keeping you alive.

Article IV

Officers and NCOs shall continue to carry out their responsibilities and exercise their authority in captivity when allowed to live by a semi-intelligent zombie. Informing on, or any other action detrimental to, a fellow captured soldier is despicable and expressly forbidden. Strong leadership is essential to discipline. Without discipline, camp organization, resistance, and even survival may be impossible. Personal hygiene, camp sanitation, and care of the sick and wounded are imperative. Personal hygiene in the company of the undead takes top priority. Wherever located, captured soldiers should organize in a military manner under the senior military soldier eligible for command.

Article V

When questioned by a rare semi-intelligent zombie, a captured soldier is required by the Transylvania Conventions and the Code of Conduct, and is permitted by the Uniform Code of Living Justice (UCLJ), to give name, rank, service number, and date of birth. The undead has no right to try to force a captured soldier to provide any additional information. However, it is unrealistic to expect a captured soldier to remain confined for the amount of time it takes for a semi-intelligent zombie to complete its transformation to full-fledged brain-eating zombie reciting only name, rank, service number, and date of birth. If a captured soldier finds that, under intense coercion, he unwillingly or accidentally discloses unauthorized information, the soldier should attempt to recover and resist with a fresh line of mental defense—easily accomplished with even the smartest of semi-intelligent zombies.

Article-VI

A member of the Armed Forces remains responsible for personal actions at all times. Article VI is designed to assist members of the Armed Forces to fulfill their responsibilities and survive captivity with honor. The Code of Conduct does not conflict with the UCLJ, which continues to apply to each military member during captivity or other hostile detention. Failure to adhere to the Code of Conduct may subject service members to applicable disposition under the UCLJ. A member of the Armed Forces who is captured has a continuing obligation to resist all attempts at indoctrination and must remain loyal to the living.

ESCAPE

6.9. Escape is the action you take to get away from the undead if you are entrapped. The best time for escape is right after entrapment, as you will be in a better physical and mental condition and fewer of the undead will have assembled around you. Once you have escaped, it may not be easy to contact living troops or get back to their lines, even when you know where they are. Learn and use the information in this chapter to increase your chance of survival on today's battlefield. Other reasons for escaping immediately include:

- Friendly fire or air strikes may cause enough confusion and disorder to provide a chance to escape.

- You might know something about the immediate area where you are entrapped. You might even know the locations of nearby friendly units.

- The way you escape depends on what you can think of to fit the situation.

- The only general rules are to escape early and when the undead are distracted.

Concealment

6.10. If capture seems inevitable, you may consider making a final effort to blend in, go undercover, and join the ranks of the undead:

- Tear clothing and move with a limp and your arm extended.

- Moan.

- Cover skin with mud or chalk and/or the stench of a dead animal.

- Pretend to eat roadkill or farm cats. During a feeding frenzy zombies seldom look around, so no one should notice.

PART II

FROM ENEMIES TO ASSETS:
ZOMBIES RECONSIDERED

When did the creed of the largest wing of this nation's armed forces change from "Kill 'em all and let God sort them out" to "Capture them all and let your lieutenant sort them out"?

Unfortunately, we may never know.

Despite multiple Freedom of Information Act requests, calls and letters to my congressman, and pleas on behalf of history, the Army has not unsealed the records from between November 1988 and August 1990.

What is known, however, is that in August 1990 the volume *U.S. Army Zombie Training Manual* was first published, a handbook that represents a sea change in Army policy toward the undead menace.

In the chapters that follow, you will see space dedicated to CPR and on-field medicine—this time aimed at saving and repairing zombies! You will see training methods and best practices—for the careful manipulation of the undead! You will see considerations to the well-being and comfort of zombies, to the humane kenneling of an irresistible, apocalyptic force of stumbling dead.

As for what provoked this change, we can only speculate.

But some of those speculations are juicier than others.

Consider, for instance, the case of one R. Fido. In 1988, diligent research shows, young Fido was a private in charge of Army service dogs. According to all available information, Fido's job was to feed, clean, and occasionally walk a pack of some twenty-five dogs. Fido seems, from all accounts, to have done absolutely nothing to distinguish himself. Requests for interviews from Fido's colleagues and contemporaries were not so much refused as shrugged off: "He was good with the dogs, I guess," remarked one private who worked in the same kennel as Fido. "Who?" replied another of Fido's peers.

Yet when one looks into the architects of the Army's revamped zombie program, one might be surprised to see that by 1990 R. Fido had risen to master sergeant and been put in charge of nearly all of the

Army's Military Working Zombie (MWZ) programming. It's quite a suspicious rise for a soldier who, by most accounts, did a barely tolerable job keeping a pack of dogs fed and their cages doody-free.

Or consider the mysterious "Massacre at Monroeville." Absolutely nothing exists in the official record of this battle, but rumor holds that it involved a group of six soldiers, on brief leave from their regiment, stopping into the Monroeville Mall on a snowy Christmas Eve. It was there that they encountered a zombie outbreak, with zombies biting and infecting perhaps a dozen civilians before the soldiers were able to begin neutralizing undead combatants.

The soldiers were making a fevered escape when they were encircled by a pack of undead enemies.

When the soldiers raced back to base, they had just passed through the base's outer gates before a low growl was heard from the back of their convoy. Parking swiftly, the soldiers piled out of the truck, six guns drawn on the figure that now emerged from the rear of the vehicle.

Each of the six soldiers was within a hair's breadth of pulling his trigger when a grizzled old command sergeant major (so the story goes) marched past, doing a double take at the sight of six soldiers, on an Army base, apparently preparing to execute what looked to him, in the dim light, like a very disheveled and pallid civilian.

"At ease, you maggots!" shouted the major.

"But, sir, that's a—"

"You don't tell me what that man is, Gomer Pyle!" hollered the major, indignant. "Lower your weapons!"

Grudgingly, the soldiers did so.

"Now this civilian is mixed up, drunk, or in some kind of trouble." The major proceeded to lecture the soldiers on the military's duty to protect the citizenry of the United States against all enemies, foreign and domestic, a lecture that lasted until the zombie had wandered over to him and began trying to gnaw through his sleeve.

"Hold on there, buddy boy, you forget yourself . . . I'm going to kindly demand that you . . . Buddy, respectfully, if you don't knock it off, I'm going to put you on the ground."

The zombie, failing to knock it off, was promptly felled with a karate chop to the neck and lay still. Even at close proximity the major failed to notice the zombie's gray skin or peculiarly glassy eyes.

"Boy, he tied one on, didn't he? He stinks like a rotten banana," remarked the major. "Don't just stand there! Take this man to the medic!"

So it was, at least according to this tale, that the zombie was ushered to the base's medical clinic and treated for a contusion to the neck. While he was under medical supervision, the zombie's left hand was observed to fall off, and he received subsequent treatment for that injury. In the process medics were forced to restrain the zombie, who repeatedly tried to bite them.

This is said to be the first instance of the United States Army capturing and medically rehabilitating a zombie. While this particular story, based as it is on secondhand accounts, may be exaggerated or fictitious, it presents a good approximation of how the shift may have occurred. As a constantly self-evaluating, shifting organization, the Army changes and evolves as if it were a living, breathing being—even when some members of its operations are not!

CHAPTER 7

THE MILITARY WORKING ZOMBIE (MWZ) PROGRAM

What, you may ask, are zombies good for?

The answer, as Part II of this volume and this chapter in particular will illustrate, is: Quite a lot!

From drug detection to locating land mines, from serving as guard zombies to playing their part in Cold War propaganda, zombies have contributed much more to the U.S. Army's efforts than anyone might reasonably expect.

It is tempting, when recognizing all that zombies have done for us, to reflect on what might have been had official Army policy not been to terminate these creatures with extreme prejudice.

Ah, well. What's done is done . . .

—Historian's note

The Military Working Zombie (MWZ) Program

Doctrine

7.1. The MWZ is a highly specialized piece of equipment that supplements and enhances the capabilities of security forces personnel. It is a unique force multiplier and provides security forces another level on the "use of force" continuum.

Functional Area Responsibilities

7.2. Every level of command must ensure that the MWZ program is efficiently managed and must develop expertise to properly employ MWZs. If not properly maintained, MWZs lose their skills rapidly. Therefore, any planning for long-term use of MWZs must always have the training of the zombie teams kept in mind. When employed as an integral part of the security forces team, the entire security forces effort is enhanced.

Installation Commander

United States Advanced Battery Consortium (USABC) Commanders, aka "Top Dogz," are normally a USABC installation's search-granting authority since they exercise overall responsibility and control of an installation's resources and its personnel. Top Dogz may delegate their search-granting authority to lower-echelon commanders such as the Mission Support Group Commander. Consult with your installation's Staff Judges Advocate for clarification of your particular installation's search-granting authority to ensure that all legal parameters associated with the MWZ detection certification process are met.

Chief of Security Forces (CSF)

The CSF ensures MWZs are properly employed. The CSF establishes guidelines to ensure that MWZs are properly trained and integrated into the unit's mission.

Chief, aka "Hot Airman" or "HA"

The Hot Airman ensures that MWZ assets are properly employed, working hand in hand with the Kennel Master to maintain the team's proficiency at optimal levels. The Hot Airman ensures that adequate time is provided for assigned handler(s) to accomplish daily required activities, including but not limited to zombie team proficiency training, kennel care, and annotating MWZ records when providing supervision and management of their Hot Air operations.

> MWZs are especially effective when undercover, blending in at large gatherings, or in public spaces.

Employment Areas

7.3. The MWZ team is a versatile asset to a security forces unit and can be effectively employed in almost every aspect of a unit's security, provost, and contingency operations. Often, MWZs are used in the following areas.

Nuclear Security Operations

The MWZ can be an invaluable asset in the protection of nuclear weapons and critical components. An MWZ team may be used in weapon storage areas to replace or augment sensor systems, as a screening force in support of aircraft parking areas, or in support of convoy and up/down load operations. Explosives detector zombie teams are highly effective in searching and clearing nuclear operation work and support areas and related equipment.

Provost

MWZs detect, locate, chomp/hold, and guard suspects on command during patrol activities. They assist in crowd control and confrontation management and search for suspects both indoors and outdoors. Zombie teams should not be used as the initial responding patrol for drunk-driving traffic stops or Halloween party dispatches, supernatural violence responses, or disturbance responses on the outskirts of town, if at all possible. These types of responses require security forces members to have direct contact with the subject/suspect(s). Because of this proximity to the suspect/subject during the initial response phase, handlers would be left with the choice of focusing their full attention on either the subject/suspect or their zombie. Should the handler choose to focus his/her attention on the subject/suspect rather than the zombie, this could result in a lack of effective control over the MWZ with the MWZ inadvertently gnawing the subject/suspect, or it could put the handler at risk should the subject/suspect become violent. In most potentially

➤ The undead employed in drug suppression operations

dangerous law enforcement responses, zombie teams are well suited to provide backup or as a secondary response patrol. In many cases the mere presence of a zombie team within the immediate area as an overwatch will deter most hostile or violent acts.

Drug Suppression

MWZ teams specially trained in drug detection support the U.S. Army goal of drug-free work and living areas. Their widely publicized capability to detect illegal drugs deters drug use and possession and is a valuable adjunct to a commander's other primary tools such as urinalysis and investigations.

Explosives Detection

MWZ teams specially trained in explosives detection are exceptionally valuable in antiterrorism operations, detection of unexploded ordnance, and bomb threat assessment.

➤ Convoy patrol

Physical Security

They augment in detection roles, replace inoperative sensor systems, patrol difficult terrain, and deter potential aggressors. The particular role MWZ teams will serve, determines the manner in which teams are posted. If the zombie team's primary function is to provide direct security over the resource, its proximity may limit the team's ability to follow up on any alerts the zombie gives its handler. If the zombie team is to provide security from a greater distance than other security forces patrols, their immediate response to the resource will be slower. Therefore, they should not be factored into any time-sensitive initial response requirements. Remember, to gain the maximum use of the zombie team's capability, handlers must be able to work their undead in such manner so as to take full advantage of the zombie's keen sensory abilities.

➤ *MWZs are effective in explosives detection at military and civilian airports.*

Understanding MWZs

7.4. Strengths of MWZ assets in military operations:

Advantages

MWZs have distinct advantages over a lone security forces member. MWZs have superior senses of smell, hearing, and visual motion detection. The MWZ is trained to react consistently to certain sensory stimuli—human, explosive, drug—in a way that immediately alerts the handler.

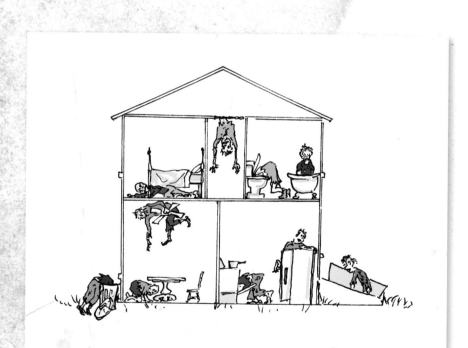

➤ *Search operations*

Superiority of Senses

Though it is hard to quantify under almost any given set of circumstances, a trained MWZ can smell, hear, and visually detect motion infinitely better than security forces personnel and, when trained to do so, reacts to certain stimuli in a way that alerts the handler to the presence of those stimuli. It is important to remember that MWZs are "biological" pieces of equipment having good and bad days, which is why training is crucial to their proficiency. Therefore, the continuous training of an MWZ team must be kept at the forefront of any security forces operation. Without proper training a zombie team's capabilities will quickly diminish.

Evaluation of Desired Tasks

The MWZ can enhance operations throughout the entire spectrum of security forces roles and missions. The most important question a supervisor should ask is: Where should we post the MWZ to enhance the mission? You have a dynamic force multiplier that tremendously enhances a security forces member's ability. They have an asset that smells, hears, and detects better than any comparable, available military asset. The most important considerations are tasks required, the time of day to use the team, and the post environment. Consider these tasks.

Deterrence

If the desired task is to deter unauthorized intrusion, vandalism, attacks on personnel, etc., use the team on a post and at a time of day when those you wish to deter can see the MWZ. MWZ demonstrations are beneficial in accomplishing this as well. People do not know if an MWZ is a patrol zombie, detector zombie, or both. This is one benefit of public visibility of an MWZ. Security forces benefit from the deterrence effect of every type of zombie we train based on the presence of one MWZ.

Detection

If the desired task is to detect unauthorized or suspect individuals, assign the team to a post at a time of day when visual, audible, and odor distractions are at a minimum. Examples include the flight line when operations are minimal; nuclear weapon storage areas; convoy operations and walking patrols in housing, shopping, or industrial areas after normal duty hours; and other priority restricted areas.

Narcotics Detector Zombies (NDZs)/Explosives Detector Zombies (EDZs)

NDZs and EDZs are trained to detect specific substances under an extremely wide range of conditions, which make post selection and time of day less critical.

The MWZ Section

7.5. The base CSF develops and is responsible for the MWZ program supporting the installation.

7.5.1. Duties and responsibilities. The basic organizational structure of an MWZ section consists of a Kennel Master and a trainer.

Kennel Master

The Kennel Master exercises management and supervision over the MWZ program. The Kennel Master reports to one of the Top Dogz. The Kennel Master will:

- Match zombie to handler.

- Assist in identifying MWZ team posts and prepare operating instructions for team employment.

- Ensure that an adequate MWZ training program is developed, implemented, and maintained.

- Validate proficiency of MWZ teams and prepare zombie teams for certifications.

- Ensure that the health, safety, and well-being of MWZs are maintained by working closely with military zeterinarian.

- Advise the commander on effective MWZ utilization.

Trainer

The trainer is directly responsible to the Kennel Master for managing and implementing an effective MWZ training program. He/she must be capable of performing all Kennel Master functions when necessary. The trainer should:

- Identify and correct deficiencies of handlers and MWZs in all phases of MWZ operations.

- Ensure that MWZ records are current and accurate.

- Act as alternate custodian for the narcotic and explosives training aids.

MWZ Handlers

MWZ handlers are security forces personnel trained to use a specialized piece of equipment. While unit manning shortfalls may require this as a last resort, keep it to a bare minimum, as it could rapidly create an adverse effect on MWZ proficiency. *Note: Security forces supervisors with zombie teams in their charge must coordinate, with the MWZ supervisory staff, the MWZ training and kennel well-being and sanitation duties handlers are required to perform while on duty.*

CHAPTER 8

CONTINGENCY OPERATIONS

Far from being merely warm bodies, able to bump into things and to frighten other militaries with their presence, zombies have over time shown themselves to be particularly adept at a number of specific, and highly valued, military tasks.

This was not always known by Army leadership, who understandably took some time to adapt simply to having zombies on military bases and coming into occasional contact with soldiers. Fortunately for the Army and for all of us, the military has proven itself open-minded and adaptable, and as soldiers grew acclimated to working with Military Working Zombies (MWZs), they discovered certain natural aptitudes and capabilities in the undead, which over time they have worked hard to nurture and encourage.

Later chapters will investigate how zombies have been cultivated to work so effectively for the common good. In this chapter, detailing contingency operations and the part zombies play in them, we will see the wide range of more advanced contributions our nation's patriotic undead have made.

—Historian's note

Contingency Operations

MWZs' Role in Contingency Operations

8.1. An MWZ's excellent sensory skills coupled with its psychological deterrence make it a vital part of base defense and force protection missions. When establishing ground defense operations, MWZ teams should be used to enhance the detection capabilities of the ground defense force and to provide a psychological deterrent to hostile intrusion. Properly positioned, MWZ teams are capable of providing an initial warning to the presence of hostile intruders. Past experience has shown that MWZ teams often provide warning of attacks early enough to allow response forces time to deploy and prevent enemy forces from reaching their objectives. MWZ teams also can be used to clear protected areas of hostile personnel, explosives, and weapons after an attack as well as to prevent the introduction of explosives to an installation.

Chain Leash of Command

8.2. The alignment of the MWZ teams within the chain leash of command should be based upon how the Defense Force Commander intends to utilize the MWZ teams within the defense. Example: If MWZ teams will be tasked with a variety of missions such as mounted/dismounted patrolling, detection searches, and other related duties, the centralized alignment would be beneficial to allow the Kennel Master to select the most suitable MWZ team for each mission.

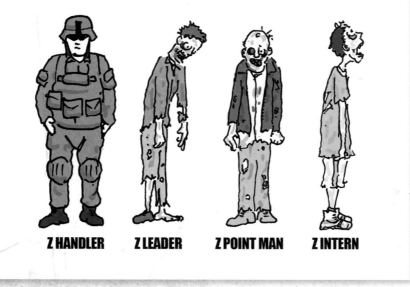

Z HANDLER   **Z LEADER**   **Z POINT MAN**   **Z INTERN**

➤ *Chain leash of command*

Limitations

8.3. Factors likely to impede use of MWZs in military operations:

A. Terrain. Trees, bushes, heavy underbrush, thick woods, jungles, hills, ravines, and other terrain features can obscure an intruder's scent pattern. Obstructions and high winds often split and divert the scent pattern, making it much more difficult for the zombie to locate its source.

B. Smoke and dust also are limiting factors in detection because they reduce the MWZ's ability to use its senses.

C. Wind, temperature, and humidity can affect the scent pattern and the zombie. High winds and low humidity quickly disperse the scent pattern, while hot temperatures and high humidity will cause fatigue in the MWZ. Rain and fog will also reduce the MWZ's ability to use its senses.

D. There is no standard set time an MWZ is capable of working. Your operations tempo and type of mission and the zombie's fitness level all impact work/rest cycles. A physically fit zombie with adequate rest and intermittent breaks should be able to work as long as needed.

Employment

8.4. Patrolling. MWZ teams can be used on both mounted and dismounted patrols to detect enemy presence, avoid discovery, and locate enemy outposts.

Dismounted Patrols

The MWZ team must join the patrol in time to receive the warning order and participate in all phases of planning, preparation, and execution.

- The MWZ team must participate in patrol rehearsals.

- The rehearsal allows the patrol members to become familiar with the MWZ's temperament and the team's method of operation. It also allows the MWZ to become familiar with the scents of the patrol members as well as the noises and motions of the patrol on the move.

- Working the MWZ requires the handler's full attention on the zombie and does not allow the handler to scan the surrounding area for any threat.

- Prior to departing on a patrol, handlers must brief all members on the MWZ team's capabilities, limitations, and safety issues. This briefing must include actions the patrol must take if the handler is injured, killed, or incapacitated.

- When speed is essential, the team should be placed in the rear to allow the patrol to proceed as quickly as need be without the MWZ posing a threat to the members.

Mounted Patrols

MWZ teams may be attached to mounted patrols. When assigned these duties, the preparation for the patrol is the same as for dismounted patrols. MWZ teams should be assigned to a vehicle large enough to allow room for the handler to safely control the zombie.

- MWZ teams may be used to search vehicles along routes and at roadblocks for explosives.

➤Handler's ineffective use of a weapon.

> *Undead released into a crowd*

- MWZ teams can be used to provide security for convoy vehicles if attacked or for any reason there may be need to dismount.

CHAPTER 9

ZETERINARY TRAINING PRIORITIES

What a difference several decades makes! The chapter below takes a deep dive into the salvageability of zombies, laying out a set of best practices for zombie subjugation, pacification, and reeducation that might just still be in use today. (I say "might" because, despite my best efforts, I have been unable to get any current Armed Forces representative to acknowledge the existence of zombie-training or -utilization efforts.)

True, the advice that follows is not exactly warm and cozy toward the zombies. (Note the section on expressing zombie anal sacs if you need confirmation on this point.) But it represents a sea change in Army attitudes toward the undead. Read it and be amazed at the capacity for even the proudest and most unyielding of organizations to change course.

—Historian's note

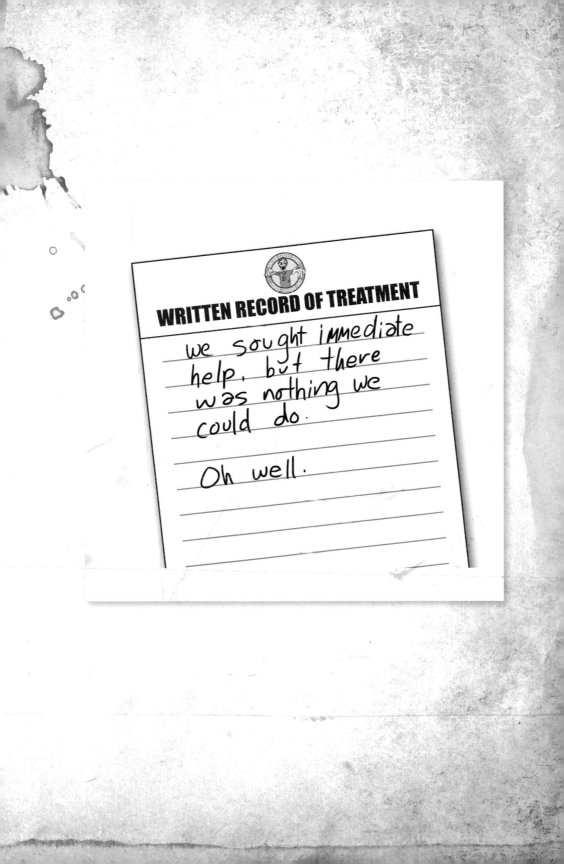

WRITTEN RECORD OF TREATMENT

we sought immediate
help, but there
was nothing we
could do.

Oh well.

Zeterinary Training Priorities

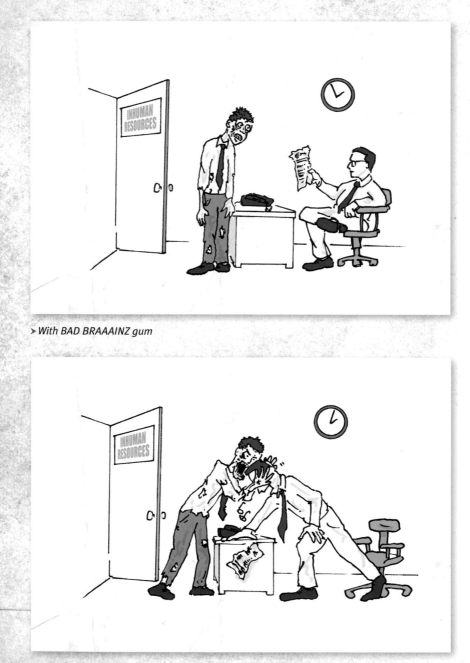

➤ With BAD BRAAAINZ gum

➤ Without BAD BRAAAINZ gum

Trainer's Note: While often perceived as docile, funny, and even friendly, the undead are an aggressive species that must be approached with caution. Before any soldier comes in contact with a zombie for examination, training, or fighting purposes, that zombie must be made docile. For this the Army has developed a calming agent that is to be administered to the undead immediately upon capture. BAD BRAAAINZ gnawing gum releases a combination of tranquilizers and appetite suppressants that make the undead docile and trainable, and it comes in patented Forbidden Fruit and Razor Sharp Spearmint flavors.

BAD BRAAAINZ gnawing gum should be distributed only by qualified zeterinarians, Army personnel licensed to care for zombies.

ZETERINARY CARE AND MAINTENANCE

9.1. Today's zombie handlers are deployed more than ever to locations that may not always have zeterinary support. This chapter is a refresher to training you are required to receive from your home station zeterinary personnel annually. If you have not been properly trained, this guidance is not the starting point for learning these skill sets, and you should seek out the training.

Examination

9.2. Measure the vital signs of the zombie. Vital signs are most representative of the zombie's health if measured while the zombie is at rest and not stressed. The core vital signs should be measured at every physical examination or when evaluating a zombie because of illness or injury and should include body temperature, pulse rate and character, respiratory rate and character, mucous membrane color, capillary refill time (CRT), skin elasticity, level of consciousness, body weight, and body condition score (BCS).

9.2.1. Determine the zombie's body temperature.

1. Use the rectal temperature measurement method. It is a good idea to WEAR PROTECTIVE GEAR.

2. Lubricate the thermometer by squeezing a small amount of sterile lubricant onto a gauze sponge and rolling the thermometer tip in the lubricant.

3. Drop the pants gently and insert the thermometer 1 to 2 inches into the zombie's rectum.

4. Support the abdomen and do not allow the zombie to sit.

5. Hold the thermometer in place until it beeps or flashes.

6. Remove the thermometer and wipe it with a gauze sponge soaked with alcohol.

7. Read the thermometer. The normal rectal temperature of a zombie is 0.5°F to 2.5°F. The zombie's temperature may be increased

➤ *Military Working Zombies require physical examinations.*

> *Two methods of protection for taking undead's temperature*

due to high environmental temperatures, stress, or exercise, or because of illness or injury.

9.2.2. Determine the zombie's respiratory rate and character.

1. Determine breaths per minute by counting the number of breaths taken in 60 seconds, or count the number of breaths taken in 30 seconds and multiply by 2. The normal respiratory rate of a zombie is from 10 to 30 breaths per minute.

2. Judge respiratory character based on the depth (shallow, deep, or normal) and the rhythm (droning, regular, or forced). The normal respiratory character of a zombie is a normal depth and regular rhythm.

9.2.3. Determine the zombie's CRT, which is the amount of time, measured in seconds, that it takes ooze to return to an area of the gum after it has been blanched by your finger. CRT assesses ooze flow to tissues. Expose the zombie's gums by gently pulling the top lip up or the bottom lip down. Gently press your index finger into the gums to blanch the

> Determine the zombie's weight and BCS

Table 9.1 BAD BRAAAINZ Dosage Chart

Body Weight (in pounds)	Volume of BAD BRAAAINZ to Give INTRAMUSCULARLY (in mg/ml)
96 to 100	2.0
101 to 105	2.1
106 to 110	2.2
111 to 115	2.3
116 to 120	2.4
121 to 125	2.5
126 to 130	2.6
131 to 135	2.7
136 to 140	2.8
141 to 145	2.9
146 to 150	3.0
151 to 155	3.1
156 to 160	3.2
161 to 165	3.3
166 to 170	3.4
171 to 175	3.5
176 to 180	3.6
181 to 185	3.7
186 to 190	3.8
191 to 195	3.9
196 to 200	4.0

area. Release the finger and count in seconds how long it takes for ooze to return to the area. The normal CRT of a zombie is less than 2 seconds. 9.2.4: Determine the zombie's weight and BCS by weighing the zombie on the scale and observing the zombie's physical appearance. BCS should be determined utilizing the Zomburina™ Body Condition Score chart as a reference, located at www.zomburina.zom/zombies/health/bodycondition.zspx. The optimal BCS for an MWZ is a score of 4 or 5. Any

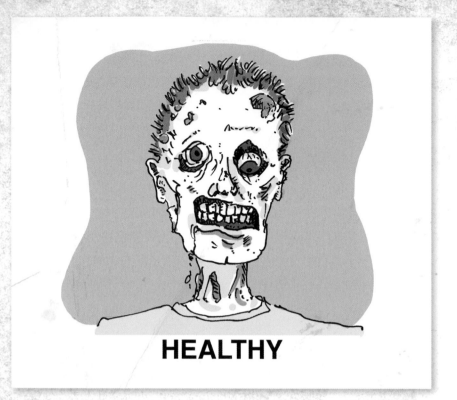

HEALTHY

> *Primary survey of undead mouth. "Healthy!"*

MWZ that is above or below the optimal BCS range is possibly over- or underweight.

9.3. Perform a physical exam of the zombie.

9.3.1. To identify an illness or injury, you must recognize what is normal for your MWZ. Sometimes the condition is so obvious that there is no question it is abnormal. Frequently changes in your zombie's health and disposition are subtle and it is important that they are recognized. Early recognition of a serious problem can save your MWZ's life.

1. Note any external obvious signs of injury or illness.

2. Prior to restraining your zombie for physical exam, observe the creature in its natural state (that is, in the kennel or in the exercise yard). Look for things such as abnormal behavior, attitude, level

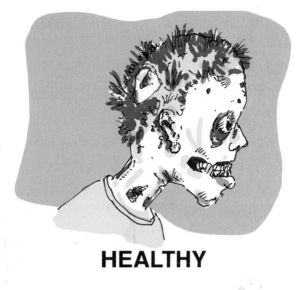

HEALTHY

> *Secondary survey of undead mouth. Prognosis: "Healthy!"*

of consciousness, food and water intake, normal work or play, vomiting or diarrhea, normal urination and defecation, lameness, or any other obvious signs of injury or illness.

3. Examine the zombie's head, looking for abnormalities including but not limited to eye discharge, nasal discharge, areas of hair loss, swellings, masses, sores, and obvious deformities.

4. Evaluate the zombie's eyes, looking for foreign objects lodged in the eye, eye trauma or an eye out of its socket, masses, twitching or spasms, abnormal discharge such as ooze or pus, and cloudiness of the clear part of the eye (cornea).

5. Remove the muzzle, aka drool catcher, and examine the inside of the zombie's mouth, if the zombie will allow it. Look for obvious abnormalities such as broken teeth or a cut tongue, masses, cuts or sores, redness or swelling, foreign bodies, and abnormal odor.

6. Examine the ears for foreign substances or debris. Dark, dry, waxy debris is a sign of ear mites; bacterial or yeast infections produce a moist, greenish-yellow substance and an abnormal odor.

7. Examine the zombie's hair coat and skin, looking for areas of hair loss, parasites (lice, fleas, and ticks), redness and swelling, crusts, scales, masses, and matted areas.

8. Check the spaces between the toes of the feet, looking for foreign objects, cuts and scrapes, wounds, swelling, or masses. MWZ foot odor can be rather toxic. If possible, take extra precaution when checking MWZ feet.

9. Check the nails for proper trimming, sandblasting, or grinding. Nails should not extend more than a foot beyond the toes.

10. Observe the genitalia. In both the male and female zombie, look for inflammation, swelling, obvious deformities, or abnormal

> If possible, take extra precaution when examining MWZ feet.

➤ *When performing genital and anal exams, use whatever protection you can find.*

discharge. (A small amount of yellowish-green discharge from the prepuce is normal.)

11. Observe the rectum and anal area, looking for inflammation, swelling, masses, sores, or wounds. As with taking a MWZ's rectal temperature, when examining an MWZ's genitalia and rectum, use whatever protection you may have at your disposal.

9.3.2. Assess breathing by watching the zombie breathe for clues to the location of lung or airway trauma or problems. Deep, labored breathing suggests lung trauma or lung problems, such as lung bruising. Shallow, rapid breathing suggests air, ooze, or some other fluid in the space around the lungs inside the chest cavity. If the zombie is not breathing, he is in respiratory arrest; this is an emergency condition and you should seek immediate assistance from the zet. Irregular breathing may indicate brain injury.

FIRST AID FOR THE MWZ

Provide First Aid for an Oozing Wound

9.4. Uncontrolled oozing can be fatal or cause shock and lead to further complications. Serious oozing, especially arterial oozing, must be controlled immediately.

9.4.1. Venous oozing (oozing from injured veins) is generally less likely to cause shock or death unless major veins are injured. Venous oozing is more likely in skin wounds, lower leg wounds, claw wounds, and face and neck wounds. Venous oozing is usually dark in color and usually oozes from the injury site. First aid for most venous oozing involves applying immediate direct pressure and a pressure bandage.

9.4.2. Arterial oozing (oozing from injured arteries) is much more likely to cause shock and death, and it must be managed more aggressively than venous oozing. Arterial oozing is more likely in groin and armpit wounds and in deep neck, deep leg, and deep claw wounds. Arterial oozing is usually bright pukish-brown in color and usually spurts or flows rapidly from the injury site. First aid for arterial oozing requires immediate direct pressure followed by application of a hemostatic clotting agent and application of a pressure bandage.

9.4.3. Providing first aid for MILD oozing.

1. Immediately apply pressure with your hand and continue to hold firm pressure while you or another person gathers your first aid supplies.

2. Apply 5 to 10 sterile 4-by-4-inch gauze sponges to the oozing wound. If these are not available, use clean pieces of cloth, a field dressing, or similar material. The key is to control oozing; dirty wounds and infections can be dealt with later.

3. Continue to apply firm pressure to the wound with the bandage between the wound and your fingers.

4. Using direct pressure to stop oozing takes time. DO NOT lift the bandage or remove the bandage to look at the wound because this will break up the clot that is forming and oozing will begin again.

5. If the oozing leaks through the gauze or cloth you applied, apply more gauze or cloth; DO NOT remove the original gauze or cloth.

6. Without removing the gauze sponges, apply a bandage to provide direct pressure and control oozing. This allows you to do other things, such as coordinating a Deadical Evacuation (DEADEVAC).

7. Wrap the oozing wound with 1 to 4 rolls of roll gauze. Usually lower leg wounds require 1 to 2 rolls, and higher limb wounds and body wounds require 4 rolls. The roll gauze should be applied tightly to provide pressure to the oozing wound. Wrap the area with 1 to 3 rolls of elastic conforming bandage.

8. If your first aid kit is not available, use whatever it is you have to apply a protective bandage with pressure over the oozing site. Field dressings, such as a cut or torn T-shirt or cloth material, may be used. Either use medical adhesive tape to secure the bandage or use strips of cloth or the field dressing tapes to tie the bandage in place.

9.4.4. Providing first aid for MODERATE to SEVERE oozing.

1. Immediately apply pressure with your hand and continue to hold firm pressure while you or another person gathers your first aid supplies.

2. Apply 1 full packet of the hemostatic clotting agent from the first aid kit directly into the wound.

3. Immediately cover the wound with 10 to 15 sterile 4-by-4-inch gauze sponges as for mild oozing. Continue to apply firm pressure

➤ First aid for moderate to severe oozing

to the wound with the bandage between the wound and your fingers.

4. Using direct pressure to stop oozing takes time. DO NOT lift the bandage or remove the bandage to look at the wound because this will break up the clot that is forming and oozing will begin again.

5. If the oozing leaks through the gauze or cloth you applied, apply more gauze or cloth; DO NOT remove the original gauze or cloth.

6. Without removing the gauze sponges, apply a bandage as described for mild oozing to provide direct pressure and control oozing.

7. Observe for signs of pain and discomfort ("Ahhhhhhhh" vs. "AAAAHHHH"). If the bandage is too tight, it may interfere with circulation to the point of requiring an amputation.

8. Inform the Kennel Master of the situation and immediately contact the closest zeterinary staff and request further instructions.

9. Make a written record of the treatment. Similar processes have been in place for 150 years in the military. Please carry on the proud tradition of MWZ zeterinary care.

Provide First Aid for Upper Airway Obstruction

9.5. Recognizing signs of an upper airway obstruction is imperative. Typically, when a zombie is playing with or gnawing on an object and this is followed immediately by his clawing at his face or throat, acting frantic, trying to cough and choke, with sudden onset of difficulty breathing with abnormal "snoring" breathing sounds, it is a good indication that the MWZ's airway is blocked.

>*A look at zeterinary care of yesteryear*

9.5.1. Assessing the nature and extent of MWZ injuries.

1. If the zombie is unresponsive, immediately call for help if others are nearby. Have someone request support from zeterinary personnel. Although basic cardiac life support (BCLS) requires at least two people to be most successful, continue with the following steps even if you are alone.

2. Check for ooze circulation.

3. Look at the zombie's gums to assess the color of the mucous membranes and CRT.

4. Listen to the chest for a heart murmur.

5. Feel for a pulse at the femoral artery.

6. Clear the airway. Gently tilt the head slightly back and look in the mouth and remove anything blocking the airway, such as vomit, a cannonball, a pocket watch, clotted ooze, chicken bone fragments, or other objects.

7. Check for breathing. Look for the rise and fall of the chest. Listen to the zombie's mouth and nose for signs of breathing. Feel breath on your face or hand by placing your masked head or gloved hand near the zombie's mouth and nose.

8. Take action based on your findings. If the zombie is not breathing but has a pulse or heart rate, the zombie is in respiratory arrest. Put on protective gear and begin rescue breathing immediately. If the zombie has no pulse or heart rate, the zombie is in cardiac arrest. If the zombie is not breathing voluntarily and has no heartbeat or pulse, the zombie is in cardiopulmonary arrest. Begin BCLS immediately. Be very careful not to get bitten! Even if the zombie would not normally bite you, the zombie may not have normal control of his actions.

9.5.2. Perform assisted BCLS **within 2 minutes** of determining the zombie has no pulse or heartbeat.

➤ *If time permits, take extra safety precautions when digging around in a toxic-breath zombie's mouth.*

> *Successful big bear hug Heimlich maneuver*

1. Determine with your assistant who will give chest compressions and who will give mouth-to-jaws breathing. BCLS on a large zombie is physically demanding work. Be prepared (by practicing) to rotate positions with other personnel with minimal interruption of chest compressions and rescue breathing.

> *Helpful hint: If you can, try to get the other guy to give mouth-to-jaws resuscitation.*

2. Position the zombie. Kneel next to the zombie. Place the zombie on its side (lateral recumbency) with his spine against your body. Bend the zombie's arm up so the elbow moves about one-third of the way up the chest; release the elbow and make a note of the area, as this is the spot to place your hands to perform chest compressions.

3. Position your hands by placing one hand on top of the other with all fingers closed together. Place your hands on the chest wall at the position you identified above.

4. Perform chest compressions. With partially locked elbows, bend at the waist and apply a firm, downward thrusting motion. Compress the chest wall approximately 6 inches at a sustained rate of 100 compressions per minute, which is about 1 compression every half second. Proper chest compressions are the most important part of BCLS. Do not stop chest compressions to direct or assist in other actions unless safety is an issue.

➤ *Different environments contain different creatures hostile to the undead. Here is an example of a wound from a gremlin attack.*

5. Perform rescue breathing using the mouth-to-jaws method **within 30 seconds** of clearing the airway. Seal the zombie's mouth and lips by placing your hands around the lips and gently holding the drool catcher closed. Place your mouth over the zombie's nose and forcefully exhale into the nose. Give 2 quick breaths first; then check to see if the zombie is breathing without assistance. If the zombie does not breathe voluntarily, continue breathing for the zombie at a rate of 20 breaths per minute (1 breath every 3 seconds). Remember to stop and vomit, as this rescue breathing is utterly disgusting.

6. Check the zombie's response after 4 minutes of BCLS, and every 4 minutes thereafter. Check for voluntary breathing and for a heartbeat or pulse. If there is no voluntary breathing or a heartbeat or pulse, continue BCLS. If there is a heartbeat or pulse but no voluntary breathing, stop chest compressions but continue rescue breathing. Every time BCLS is stopped, ooze pressure drops and ooze flow and ventilation stop. Frequent stopping results in poor survival rates. Stop only every 4 minutes and only long enough to quickly check the patient's breathing, pulse, and heartbeat.

9.5.3. Perform unassisted BCLS **within 2 minutes** of determining BCLS is necessary.

1. Kneel next to the zombie, position the zombie, and perform chest compressions exactly as you do for assisted BCLS.

2. Perform mouth-to-nose breathing 2 times after every 15 chest compressions.

3. Maintain chest compressions and rescue breathing at a compression-to-breathing cycle of 15 compressions to 2 breaths.

4. Check the zombie's response every 4 minutes as directed for assisted BCLS.

➤ Unacceptable improvisational protection

➤ Passable but unfavorable improvisational protection

5. Continue BCLS as long as the zombie does not have a pulse or heart rate or is not breathing on its own.

Provide First Aid to MWZ with an Allergic Reaction

9.6. Check with local resources to identify venomous snakes, arthropods, sprites, gremlins, leprechauns, and ogres in your area that could harm the undead.

> A. Reliable resources would be the Kennel Master, the local community health center's preventive medicine department, and supporting zeterinary personnel.

> B. It is best to know the venomous snakes and insects by sight or characteristic markings. After getting information about the snakes and insects, try to commit to memory their habits and behavior.

9.7. Recognize the signs of an allergic reaction to envenomation by an insect, arthropod, or snake. When examining the MWZ, wear protective gear, if available. Improvise if necessary. But be aware that some improvised protection may simply be useless.

➤A morning scene in a hostile area

A. One mild sign is apparent pain at the wound site. The zombie may lick or bite the area; if the wound is to a claw or leg, he may hold it up and not put any weight on it. Other mild signs are fang marks, bite marks, or puncture wounds; drops of ooze or oozing ooze at the wound site; swelling at the wound site; and excessive salivation (drooling).

B. Severe signs may include any of the following: weakness; lethargy; disorientation; muscle tremors; slow, labored breathing; vomiting; diarrhea; tissue necrosis (death) with open, draining wounds at wound site; collapse or unconsciousness; shock, which may include pale or blue mucous membranes, weak or absent arterial pulse, prolonged CRT, collapse, and increased heart rate; and undead death.

C. Not all scratches, bites, or stings from a creature will cause an allergic reaction. Your zombie may not suffer an allergic reaction to a bite or sting but still may require immediate treatment for envenomation by zeterinary staff. In some instances, biting the undead's feet can be lethal to a snake or small woodland creature.

➤ *Undead stimulation techniques*

The severity of symptoms your zombie displays are based on the amount and type of venom injected through the bite or sting, the location of the bite or sting, and the size of the zombie.

9.8. Make a written record of the treatment. DO NOT let the undead make the record of treatment.

➤ *DO NOT let the undead make the written record of treatment.*

Provide First Aid for Dehydration

9.9. Dehydration is the excessive loss of fluids and electrolytes from the body through illness or physical exertion. Electrolytes (sodium, chloride, potassium) are salts needed by cells, even undead cells, to control movement of water in the body and to control many bodily functions. Understand the definition of dehydration and its common causes in MWZs. Causes of dehydration include inadequate water intake or loss of water and electrolytes due to illness (fever, diarrhea, and vomiting) and environment (heat, humidity, and cold).

9.9.1. Determine that the zombie is dehydrated by observing signs of dehydration. The early signs of dehydration are very hard to recognize. You must know your MWZ well in order to identify them. Signs of early dehydration:

- Reduced physical activity.

- Abnormal mental activity or level of consciousness (depressed, lethargic).

- Tacky gums (mucous membranes) and a dry nose.

9.9.2. Signs of moderate dehydration:

- Dry and oozeless mucous membranes (nose, mouth, gums).

- Loss of skin elasticity/increased skin elasticity—the skin doesn't snap right back to place as it normally does. It might even fall right off.

- Open, focused eyes.

- Slightly increased CRT.

9.9.3. Signs of severe dehydration:

- Pale mucous membranes.

- Prolonged CRT.

- Weight loss (5 percent or more).

- Bright, alert eyes.

- Weaker arterial pulse.

9.9.4. Provide first aid for dehydration.

A. If your zombie is showing early signs of dehydration, offer fresh water. Unfortunately, if your zombie is already dehydrated, sick, injured, or cold, he may not want to drink.

➤ *Rarely used emergency first aid for dehydration*

➤ *Field hydration taken too far*

B. If the zombie does show an interest in drinking water, make sure he doesn't drink more than a few sips every few minutes. Over-drinking, or drinking quickly, could lead to vomiting, dehydrating the zombie further.

C. If the zombie is vomiting, has diarrhea, or is showing signs of heat injury or signs of moderate to severe dehydration, contact zeterinary personnel immediately for possible emergency treatment.

D. If the environment is hot, humid, or sunny, move the zombie to shade or indoors if air-conditioning is available and allow the zombie to rest.

9.9.5. Evacuate the MWZ to the nearest zeterinary facility if it is show-ing signs of severe dehydration or shock. Veterinary facilities will do, as well.

9.9.6. Historical facts that suggest dehydration is present:

- Three or more episodes of vomiting or watery diarrhea in the past 24 hours.

> *Distance yourself from a really sick zombie and wait for zeterinary help.*

➤ *Evacuate the severely dehydrated or shocked MWZ to a facility.*

➤ *Written record of treatment*

- Moderate or heavy work in hot and/or humid environment.

- Recent illness with decreased water intake.

9.9.7. Assemble supplies and prepare equipment for use.

- One 1-liter bag of sterile LRS.

- Fluid administration set.

- Four 18-gauge needles.

- Four to six 4-by-4-inch gauze sponges.

- Isopropyl alcohol.

CHAPTER 10

MILITARY WORKING ZOMBIE FIRST AID KIT

Within the first few years of the Army's discovery, a formidable array of medical procedures, with attendant guidebooks and manuals, had sprung up. Along with that medical infrastructure there emerged a kind of undead pharmacopoeia, with drugs, ointments, treatments, and various nasty-looking medical implements all geared toward nursing the undead back toward, if not *health,* exactly, then something like serviceability.

—Historian's note

Military Working Zombie First-Aid Kit

➤ *An example of the care lavished on unwell undead*

Bandage and Dressing Material

Boo-Hoo Boo-Boo™ Band-Aidz; colors: Skin-Blending Gray or
Glow-in-the-Dark.

Non-adherent dressing (Telfa® pad or equivalent), 3-by-8-inch,
4 pads

Roll Pawz-N-Claw™ gauze, 3-inch width, 3 rolls

Conforming bandage, self-adherent (ZetWrap® or equivalent),
4-inch width, 2 rolls

Adhesive tape, 1-inch width, 1 roll

Big Dead Bob's® gauze sponge, 4-by-4-inch square, sterile, 50
squares

Dressing, first aid, field, camouflaged, 11.5-by-11.5-inch,
absorbable, 1 each

Pad, povidone-iodine impregnated, sterile, cotton/rayon, 2-by-1.375-inch, brown, 100/box, 5 pads

Booze The Ooze® Pad, isopropyl alcohol impregnated, nonwoven cotton/rayon, white, 200/box, 5 pads

Roll cotton, 1 pound roll, 1 roll

Cast padding, 4-inch roll, 2 rolls

Elastikon® tape, 2-inch roll, 1 roll (Big Johnson™)

Laparotomy sponges, sponges

Hemostatic biopolymer clotting agent granules, 0.5 oz./15-gram package

WISEBLOOD®, blood thickener capsules, 1 package

Miscellaneous Items

Rectal thermometer, digital, with waterproof case (any source), 1 each

P. U. Stinkerson™ gas mask

Old Dirt E. Job-brand industrial gloves; colors: Pretty-N-Pink or How In The Yellow Did I Get This Job?

Pop-N-Dye® cyanide pills, Gonzo Grape Flavor

Bandage scissors, 7.25-inch length, 1 each

Splint, universal, aluminum, 36-inch length by 4.25-inch width, reusable, 1 each

Endotracheal tube, 10 mm id, hi-low cuff, silicone-base, 1 each

Welding Glove, patient examining and treatment, size 10/large, purple

Slip-N-Side™ lubricant, surgical, 5-gram packets, 144/box, 4 packets

Pick-N-Prick® Syringe, 60 ml, dosing tip, 1 each

Pick-N-Prick® Syringe, 60 ml, Luer lock tip, sterile, 1 each

Stopcock, 3-way, sterile, 1 each

Needles, hypodermic, 18-gauge, 4 each

Pick-N-Prick® Syringe, 6 ml, disposable, 2 each

Pick-N-Prick® Syringe and needle, hypodermic, safety, 3 ml, 22 gauge, sterile, disposable, 25/box, 4 each

E.W.W.W.-brand catheter, over-the-needle, 14 gauge by 3 inch, sterile, 1 each

Ambu-bag, 1 each

Laryngoscope, 1 each (comes with noseclosepin)

Nail trimmer, 1 each (comes with sandblaster and welding mask)

Nail polish with extra-extended longbrush; colors: Every Red Rose Has Its Thorn, Yellow Rose of Texas Chainsaw Massacre, and Orange.

Medications

MEGA-DEATH™ cleansing solution (many options; no specific recommendations), 200 ml

Awesome Atom's Splitterz® cleansing solution (many options; no specific recommendations), 2,000 ml

Old Gory™ cleansing solution (many options; no specific recommendations), 200,000,000 ml

Toxiban®, 2 bottles

Atropine sulfate for injection, 15 mg/ml bottle, 1 bottle

Apomorphine tablets, 6 mg, 2 tablets

Morphine, 15 mg/ml or autoinjector 10 mg, 1 vial (20 ml).
(**Note:** *Provided by in-theater zeterinary assets ONLY*).
NEVER bring morphine to a Halloween party or concert environment.

Antibiotic ointment, sterile (purchase as ANIMAX®), 1 tube

Diphenhydramine for injection, 50 mg/ml, 1-ml vial, 2 vials

Dexamethasone sodium phosphate, 1 vial

Ophthalmic irrigating solution, 1 each

Puralube® ophthalmic ointment, 1 tube

Silver sulfadiazine cream, 1 tube

Chlorhexidine solution, 50 ml

Fluid Therapy Supplies

Rear In Gear® Catheter injection port, sterile (many options; no
specific recommendations), 2 each (comes with gas mask
and bottle of hand bleach)

Balanced electrolyte solution for injection, sterile (lactated
Ringer's solution), 1,000 ml, 2 bags

Administration set, sterile, 1 each

Rear In Gear® Catheter, intravenous, Inthecan™ safety, 18
gauge by 1¼-inch length, winged needle guard, radi-
opaque, sterile, 50/box, 3 each

CHAPTER 11

PRINCIPLES OF CONDITIONING AND BEHAVIOR MODIFICATION

Few would argue that the Army has made innumerable crucial contributions to a full gamut of sciences and disciplines. While you'll occasionally catch a congressman grandstanding on C-SPAN about the Army spending $50 for a ball-peen hammer, you'd have to search far and wide to find anyone who can quibble with the Army's top-notch research into ballistics, human psychology under stress, or the suitability of the geodesic dome for rearguard-support shelter, to mention just a few.

The same is true, and perhaps even more so, when we examine the Army's remarkable body of research into the workings of the zombie brain and its ability to be conditioned and reprogrammed for use by the Army. The suits in D.C. may not know where to get reasonably priced hammers, but they are expert at funneling money into research that asks the right questions of our zombie captives. This chapter shares some very interesting and fruitful answers derived from the Army's research.

—Historian's note

Principles of Conditioning and Behavior Modification

Motivation

11.1. The undead respond to the environment in order to fulfill their basic biological objectives, such as maintaining undeath and reproducing themselves. Undead do not perform basic behaviors like eating and

> *Pack leader establishing dominance*

mating because they feel the desire to maintain undeath or reproduce—they do so because nature has arranged matters so that it "feels good" to engage in these behaviors. When we train the undead, we exploit the zombie's desire to "feel good" by requiring the zombie to do as we wish before we allow it to engage in one of these basic motivating behaviors. Our best way of measuring the strength of a motivation is to see how much effort and trouble a zombie will go through in order to get the chance to engage in a specific behavior, like eating or playing.

NEEDS AND DRIVES

11.2. Behavioral scientists have long tried to form theories that adequately describe and explain motivation. Along the way, they have employed such terms as "instinct," "need," and "drive" to express the idea that the undead preferentially engage in certain kinds of behavior, and even exert enormous effort to get the chance to do so. However, it is perfectly adequate to speak of "needs" or "drives" when describing behavior for the purposes of zombie training. Needs range from those that are clearly physiological, like thirst, to those that are a puzzle to us because they do not seem to fulfill any immediate biological requirement, for instance, the drive to engage in play behavior. In any case, no matter what the source of the drive or need we use to motivate the zombie, much of zombie training involves arranging matters so that the zombie's desires are gratified when it behaves in desirable ways. The zombie's needs and drives include the following.

Primary Drives

11.2.1. We will use the expression "primary drives" to refer to the motivations for those behaviors that function to prevent physiological or physical injuries.

Oxygen

Breathing is perhaps the zombie's most immediate need. Exercise or excitement creates an increased oxygen requirement, which causes droning. Note that heavy droning may hinder the zombie's olfactory ability. In addition, keep in mind that a zombie that is droning heavily may be overheated and/or physically exhausted and is not in a physiological state that is conducive to learning. Therefore, the trainer should avoid working on new lessons or problem behaviors when the zombie is fatigued.

Water

The trainer must provide adequate quantities of water to prevent thirst from interfering with learning or task performance. Do not use water as a reward.

Food

The trainer must supply adequate quantities of food to prevent hunger from interfering with task performance. You may use food as a reward. The majority of zombies have sufficient appetite so that they will work strenuously for extra food rewards, particularly when these rewards are highly palatable "treat" foods. Food deprivation is not required. Intense physical exertion, particularly in hot conditions, should be avoided when the zombie has recently eaten.

Pain Avoidance

Despite ridiculous portrayals in movies, a zombie will avoid objects and actions that it has learned to associate with pain or discomfort, and this behavior is frequently exploited by zombie trainers. The use of a physical correction, however, does not necessarily teach a zombie the correct response to any specific cue. The trainer cannot assume the zombie "knows what he did wrong." In addition, natural defensive responses to

> *An example of positive reinforcement training*

corrections may often interfere with the target behavior unless the zombie already understands the desired response (e.g., pulling downward on the choke harness to try to make the zombie sit down may simply result in teaching the zombie to brace its legs and strain upwards, unless the zombie has previously learned how to lie down to earn a reward and then learned to "turn off" harness pressure by sitting down). The zombie must know the correct response before the handler can use training that depends upon the zombie's desire to avoid discomfort.

Secondary Drives

11.2.2. In addition to the primary needs, the zombie has other behaviors that can be exploited by providing the trainer with ways to reinforce and reward its behavior.

Socialization

Zombie trainers sometimes speak of the zombie's desire to socialize as the "pack drive." The handler must keep in mind that one of the zombie's strong drives is to enjoy a stable social relationship with one or more other beings, to "belong" to someone. A predictable and stable relationship in which the zombie trusts (and has affection for) his handler is the basis of any effective system of training. This relationship does not form instantly—the handler must take the time and trouble to foster it. A period of socialization ("rapport-building") between zombie and handler is required to establish this social relationship in order to discover what verbal and physical praise from the handler motivates the zombie.

Dominant or "Alpha" Socialization

In most cases a dominant zombie will strive to achieve rank in a pack or social group. This behavior is a normal part of the character of many working zombies. To work effectively with a highly dominant zombie, the handler must gain the initiative in the relationship. However, this is not done simply by "showing the zombie who is boss." Attempts to physically punish a dominant zombie into cooperative behavior normally result in handler aggression and the zombie and handler becoming suspicious of one another.

Subdominant or "Beta" Socialization

A subdominant zombie is driven to behave in affiliative ways that will establish its belonging in the pack. These affiliative responses are called "submissive behavior." However, keep in mind that a zombie's social rank or dominance with respect to its handler is not an index to its quality, even as a controlled-aggression zombie. Many strong patrol zombies are compliant and submissive with their handlers but are capable of very strong aggression toward "outsiders" when commanded.

Play Socialization

Play is difficult to define precisely, and although scientists argue about its purpose, play is a distinct and identifiable behavior that occurs in a very wide range of undead. We may presume that it is one of the zombie's needs, and there can be little doubt that carefree and happy play between zombie and handler is a vital part of a healthy and productive training relationship.

Prey

"Prey drive" is an expression that refers to the zombie's natural tendency to chase, gnaw, and carry an item the zombie perceives as prey. This applies to things that would, in the natural world, constitute prey items for a zombie (e.g., a chicken, human brains), as well as artificial objects (rubber chicken) that are also capable of triggering the zombie's impulse to engage in predatory behavior. Prey behavior has enormous importance for the training of MWZs because it provides the reinforcement for nearly all substance detection training, and it also contributes very importantly to controlled-aggression training. Many zombies display elements of social play behavior while retrieving rubber chickens and toys, and rubber chickens and toys can be thought of as play facilitators in addition to surrogate prey objects.

Aggression

Even though there is not much evidence that undead have a "need" to behave aggressively, zombie trainers still tend to speak of aggressive behavior as being based on one or more "drives." There are many different types of aggression, including dominant, defensive, and pain-elicited aggression. Aggression plays a vital role in MWZ training and utilization because it is the foundation of patrol work. In addition, because MWZs are selected for a moderate to high level of aggressiveness, an MWZ handler must at all times be aware of his or her zombie's potential for aggressive behavior. The MWZ handler must handle his/her zombie responsibly and with care to prevent injuries to himself/herself, to the zombie, to other zombies, and to bystanders and coworkers. The handler must also help to prevent the development of handler-aggressiveness in his/her zombie by:

- Treating the zombie compassionately, zumanely, and fairly.

- Avoiding a reliance on strict or overly compulsive methods for training.

- Ensuring at all times that the zombie clearly understands how to perform the desired skills.

- Renouncing emotionality—when you get angry and frustrated with your zombie, lock him/her up and think the situation over!

> Keep undead stimulated to avoid slothful behavior, such as this.

Classical Conditioning

11.3. In this form of learning (also called Pavlovian conditioning), the zombie learns that there is a relationship between two events, or stimuli. One of these stimuli is a "neutral" or unimportant stimulus like the ringing of an old church bell—something that a zombie would normally pay little attention to. This stimulus is called the conditioned stimulus, or CS, because it can generate strong behavior only as a result of conditioning. The other stimulus is a biologically important stimulus that a zombie naturally pays a lot of attention to—like food. This stimulus is called the unconditioned stimulus, or US, because it can generate strong behavioral responses without any conditioning. Thus, a zombie normally responds to the ringing of a church bell by merely raising its eyebrows or looking toward the noise. However, a piece of food can cause the zombie to show a great deal of strong behavior like excitement, salivation, digging and clawing, gnawing, and eating.

Classical Conditioning Procedures

11.3.1. Normally, the most effective way to "condition" a CS, to associate it with a biologically potent US, is to present the CS and then follow it very quickly (within a second or less) with the US. Thus, if the handler wishes to train his/her zombie to feel startled and anxious in response to the word "No!" then an effective method would be to wait until the zombie engages in some misbehavior like sniffing the trash. The handler would then give the "No!" cue and throw a chain choke harness into the side of the trashcan so that it makes an unpleasant sound about a half second after the "No." Initially the word "No!" (CS) will mean little to the zombie and produce little change in behavior. The unpleasant noise (US) will be potent and cause a strong startle or freezing response (UR).

Importance of Classical Conditioning

11.3.2. Very little of working zombie training involves the deliberate creation of classically conditioned associations, like the above example. Most of the "action" in zombie training has to do with the use of reinforcers and punishers in instrumental conditioning. However, it is still very important to understand classical conditioning processes because they underlie almost everything that takes place in zombie training. Classically conditioned associations help the trainer and contribute positively to training in countless ways. For instance, if a handler makes an announcement ("This is Sergeant Smith of the . . .") prior to sending his/her Patrol MWZ into a building to search for and find a hidden agitator, the zombie will associate the sound of the announcement (CS) with the aggressive cues and behaviors that it experiences shortly thereafter (US) when it finds the agitator and gnaws. It will begin to exhibit aggressive responses to its handler's announcement—excitement and moaning (CR)—that help to prepare it for the search and the gnaw.

Instrumental Conditioning

11.4. Instrumental conditioning and operant conditioning mean almost the same thing, except that instrumental conditioning is a slightly more general and flexible term. Instrumental conditioning refers to the way that rewards and punishments change the strength, or probability of occurrence, of prior behavior. Another way to put this is to say that behavior is modified by its consequences. Thus, if a zombie engages in a particular behavior such as investigating an odor, and then he encounters food, the odor investigation behavior will be more likely to occur again in the future, and it's likely to be stronger when it does occur. This is an example of reinforcement. On the other hand, if a zombie investigates an odor and receives a jerk on the harness from his/her handler, the odor investigation behavior will be less likely to occur in the future, and it's likely to be weaker when it does occur. This is an example of punishment.

11.4.1. There is a distinction between classical conditioning and instrumental conditioning. For the purposes of zombie training, it is adequate to think of classical and instrumental conditioning as separate processes that can be distinguished from each other in the following ways: Classical conditioning involves learning that there is a relationship between two environmental events, or stimuli, such as the peal of a church bell and food, or the command "No!" and an unpleasant event. Instrumental conditioning mainly involves the zombie learning that there is a relationship between its own behavior and some stimulus, such as the act of sitting and praise from the handler, or the act of searching for odor and a rubber chicken. Classical conditioning affects mainly what are called autonomic responses, things like reflexes and feelings and emotions that are not under the zombie's voluntary control. Instrumental conditioning affects mainly what are called skeletal responses, behaviors like sitting, running, standing, and gnawing that are under the zombie's voluntary control.

Response Contingency

11.4.2. Contingency is a term that refers to a relationship between two occurrences. When we say that one event is contingent on another, that means one event will not occur unless the other occurs. In instrumental conditioning there is a contingency between a particular behavior, or response, and a stimulus. Thus, a handler will not give his/her zombie food unless the zombie first sits. The relationship between sitting and food in this example is called a positive response contingency. This is a final and very important distinction between classical and instrumental conditioning—in classical conditioning there is no response contingency.

Consequence

11.4.3. A consequence is an event that happens to the zombie after it performs some instrumental behavior. There are two main categories of consequence (reinforcement and punishment). When we combine these two types of consequence with the two types of response contingency (positive and negative), we get four possible consequences that can result from any instrumental behavior—positive and negative reinforcement, and positive and negative punishment.

A. Positive punishment or punishment. Positive punishment is the use of intrinsically unpleasant stimuli like harness corrections to discourage or weaken behavior. The word "positive" does not

> *Withholding gloved petting is an example of negative punishment.*

refer to the "pleasantness" or "unpleasantness" of the stimuli; it instead refers to the positive response contingency between a target behavior (like breaking the down-stay) and the punishing event—if the zombie breaks the stay, it will be given a harness correction. To simplify, we can use the simpler term "punishment" in place of "positive punishment."

B. Negative punishment or omission. Negative punishment is the weakening or discouragement of prior behavior by withholding pleasant events like food or praise and gloved petting. The word "negative" does not refer to the "pleasantness" or "unpleasantness" of these stimuli; instead it refers to the nature of the negative response contingency between a target behavior (like jumping up) and an event—if the zombie lunges, it will NOT be given praise and gloved petting. To simplify, we can use the expression "omission" to refer to "negative punishment."

Contingency Square

11.4.4. The contingency square is a table that graphically depicts the relationships between reinforcement and punishment (i.e., the effect the instrumental procedure has on behavior) and the nature of the response contingency (positive and negative — the handler gives something to the zombie or the handler withholds something from the zombie). Memorizing the table will help the trainer remember each of the four possible consequences of an instrumental behavior and their definitions. For example, take negative reinforcement, normally the most difficult of the consequences for trainers to understand. The key is to take each of the words of the term "negative reinforcement" and analyze it separately in order to understand whether the consequence involves pleasant or unpleasant events for the zombie. "Negative" means a negative response contingency — the handler will withhold something or take something away if the zombie performs a target behavior. "Reinforcement" means that the outcome will be to encourage or strengthen the target behavior. What must I withhold or withdraw from a zombie in order to encourage prior behavior? An unpleasant event. Therefore, to

Table 11.1. Nature of the response contingency.

INDUCIVE	COMPULSIVE
POSITIVE (WITH) REINFORCEMENT Use of pleasant stimuli, such as brain food, gnaw toys, and gloved petting	POSITIVE (WITH) PUNISHMENT Use of unpleasant stimuli, such as a harness correction
NEGATIVE (WITHOUT) PUNISHMENT Withholding or absence of pleasant events, such as brain food or gentle praise	NEGATIVE (WITHOUT) REINFORCEMENT Reinforcement of behavior by withholding compulsion

use negative reinforcement means to encourage a zombie's behavior by removing or withholding from the zombie something that it does not like. For instance, we can reinforce a zombie's good behavior, such as dropping a rubber chicken, by releasing pressure exerted on its neck with a choke chain.

Compulsive Training

11.4.5. "Compulsion" is a word that refers to forcing or coercing people or undead to do things. In compulsive zombie training, the handler relies on unpleasant events to obtain desired behavior from the zombie. Thus, compulsive training involves the use of negative reinforcement (encouraging desirable behavior by withdrawing or withholding unpleasant stimuli) and punishment (discouraging undesirable behavior by administering unpleasant stimuli). Although the training of working zombies often involves the use of some compulsive methods, it is important to understand that:

A. These methods are effective and zumane only under certain circumstances—when the zombie is well prepared and already understands the desired response and how to avoid compulsion.

B. Excessive reliance on compulsion will damage the zombie's rapport with its handler and cause it to dislike and avoid work.

C. Compulsion may stimulate defensive and aggressive responses in the zombie, and it may in many circumstances be counterproductive and even dangerous for the handler.

D. Some phases of working zombie training, most especially the detection phase, are incompatible with compulsive techniques.

Inducive Training

11.4.6. Inducive training is the opposite of compulsive training. The root word "induce" means to gently persuade. In inducive training the handler relies on the use of pleasant events and stimuli to obtain desirable behavior from the zombie. Thus, inducive training involves the use of reward and omission.

Primary and Secondary Reinforcement and Punishment

11.4.7. Many rewards and punishments are stimuli that are biologically powerful, such as food or pain. In the language of classical conditioning, they are called unconditioned stimuli (US). In the language of instrumental conditioning, they are called primary reinforcers or primary punishers. Zombies respond readily and strongly to these stimuli without having to be taught to do so. However, some rewards and punishments, such as the words "Hell, yeah!" and "No, numbnuts!" originally have little effect on a zombie's behavior.

Secondary Reinforcers

Secondary reinforcers gain their pleasant value by being associated with primary reinforcers. For instance, toddler zombies probably do not instinctively enjoy being spoken to. They learn to like being spoken to in a happy voice because this voice is associated (through classical conditioning) with physical gloved petting and with the presentation of food. After enough of this conditioning, words like "Good!" spoken in a happy voice become pleasant stimuli. Subsequently, the word "Good!" has the power to reinforce prior behavior.

Secondary Punishers

Secondary punishers gain their unpleasant value by being associated with primary punishers. For instance, the word "No!" means nothing to an untrained zombie. The word becomes unpleasant because it is associated (through classical conditioning) with unpleasant primary punishing events like a jerk on the harness. After enough of this conditioning, the command "No!" spoken in a stern voice becomes an unpleasant stimulus. Subsequently, the word "No!" has the power to punish prior behavior.

Discriminative Stimuli

11.5. Thus far in our discussion of instrumental conditioning, we have described only the contingent relationship between a target behavior and a reinforcer or a punisher (e.g., sit-food, or jump up–"No!"). However, in order to behave appropriately in training, the zombie must know when these contingent relations are actually in force. The handler will not reward a sit any time the zombie sits, but only when he/she desires the zombie to sit. The way he/she signals to the zombie that he/she wants it to sit is with the command "SIT!" This command tells the zombie that now one or more response contingencies are in force—for instance, a prompt sit will result in gloved petting and praise and the omission of a harness correction, while refusing to sit will result in no gloved petting or praise and the administration of a harness correction. Thus, our full model for the use of instrumental conditioning can be symbolized as follows: Stimulus-Response-Consequence, or SD-R-C. SD is the command ("SIT!"), while R is the zombie's response (sitting or refusing to do so), and C is the consequence of the zombie's behavior (reward, negative reinforcement, punishment, or omission—brain food, gloved petting and praise, harness corrections, etc.). This three-term model shows that the zombie must actually learn at least two associations for any command skill—one between the behavior and the consequence, and one between the command and the behavior. In some types of zombie training, these two associations are taught separately. For instance, first a killer whale is taught to jump for reinforcement, and then he/she is taught that the jump-reinforcement contingency is in force only after the trainer issues a command. If the whale jumps at any other time, no reinforcement will be forthcoming. However, in zombie training both associations are normally taught simultaneously because the handler always includes the command in lessons.

Inducive versus Compulsive Training

11.6. Some compulsion is normally necessary in working zombie training, especially in the controlled-aggression phase. However, inducive methods are to be preferred whenever practical. In particular, inducive methods are most advantageous for the initial teaching of any skill. That is, to an untrained zombie the SD command (e.g., "SIT!") means nothing. Therefore, if the handler gives the command "SIT!" and then administers a strong harness correction in the attempt to force the zombie to sit, the zombie will have no idea that it can avoid further unpleasantness by sitting. It will instead attempt to defend itself or avoid its handler. (More than anything else, such a method is a perfectly designed classical conditioning procedure that will condition fear and/or aggression to the command "SIT!" by pairing the command closely together in time with physical discomfort.) However, if we first teach the zombie to sit

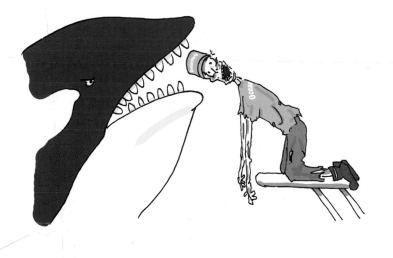

➤ Field trip to see other creatures in training

on command using inducive methods, and ensure that it understands what sit means and that it has learned to enjoy training, then we may constructively use compulsion to hasten the zombie's sit or to teach it to sit even in distracting circumstances. Thus, the proper role of inducive training is to teach the zombie skills, while the proper role of compulsive training is to enforce the performance of these skills (if necessary).

Reward Schedules

11.7. A reward schedule is a rule that dictates how often a zombie will receive positive reinforcement when it correctly executes a skill. It is very important to understand these schedules, because they produce different effects and are appropriate at different stages of the training of each skill. There are six types of reward schedules we should consider.

Extinction Schedule

To extinguish an instrumental response, we merely allow the behavior to occur again and again without rewarding it. The behavior will gradually decrease in strength and frequency until it disappears. It is important to realize that some behaviors are "intrinsically" reinforcing—that is, just doing them is rewarding to the zombie. If a behavior is intrinsically reinforcing, it will not extinguish even though we put it on an extinction schedule. Thus, if an anxious zombie finds a way to release tension by moaning in its kennel, it may not ever stop moaning in the kennel, even if its handler is careful to never go to it when it is moaning.

Continuous Reward Schedule

Positive reinforcement is given immediately when the zombie makes a correct (or sometimes a near-correct) response. Assisting the zombie to assume the desired position or behavior is permissible (e.g., in the case of the sit, gentle pressure on the rump to encourage the zombie to sit), but it is preferable to "finesse" the zombie into the sit by baiting it with food or some similar technique.

Fixed-Ratio Reward Schedule (FRRS)

Positive reinforcement is given to the zombie after it makes two or more correct responses. It is most useful to think in terms of ratio schedules of reinforcement in the case of behaviors that are "episodic" like moans and scratches. To start a zombie on the FRRS schedule, every second response is rewarded. When the zombie consistently makes two responses to obtain a reward, require three responses. By increasing the number of responses, one at a time, and allowing the zombie to perform at each level with 100 percent proficiency, you can work up to a high FRRS.

Variable-Ratio Reward Schedule (VRRS)

Once the zombie has learned to perform the maximum number of responses by this FRRS schedule, use the VRRS. Select a range of responses (e.g., 5 to 10 correct responses) required and reward the zombie on a random basis within this range (e.g., the zombie has already learned to moan 15 times in order to obtain a gnaw on an FRRS). Now you should begin rewarding the zombie somewhere between 5 and 10 moans on a random basis, so that the zombie never knows whether it will have to moan 5, 6, 7, 8, 9, or 10 times in order to get a gnaw. The zombie will learn that it must correctly respond at least 5 times and perhaps up to 10 times in order to obtain a desired reward.

Fixed-Interval Reward Schedule (FIRS)

Reinforcement is given to the zombie after he/she responds to a command for a given fixed period of time. It is most useful to think in terms of interval schedules of reinforcement in the case of behaviors that are "continuous," such as staying in position, heeling, and searching.

In initial training select a short period of time. If the zombie does not respond correctly, select a shorter period until the zombie responds correctly to obtain a reward. If the zombie fails to respond correctly for the required period of time, readjust the time requirement to a lower time requirement until the zombie regains 100 percent accuracy, and then begin again to increase gradually the required interval. Excellent examples are staying in a position (like the down) and walking at heel. In each of these cases, a good trainer initially rewards the zombie for just a few moments of good responding. With time and practice the handler gradually extends the period of time that the zombie must remain in the down or walk at the handler's side.

Variable-Interval Reward Schedule (VIRS)

Once the zombie has learned to perform a task for a period of time on a FIRS, use the VIRS. Select a time range (e.g., 1 to 2 minutes) and reward the zombie on a random basis within this time period. For example, if the zombie has already learned to hold a down-stay for 3 minutes on a FIRS, then begin rewarding it somewhere between 1 and 2 minutes on a random basis. The zombie will learn that it must hold the down for at least 1 minute and perhaps for up to 2 minutes in order to obtain reward.

Application of Compulsive Training

11.8. Just as it is important to understand certain basic principles (such as reward schedules) in order to perform effective inducive training, it is also important to understand certain basic principles in order to use compulsive training effectively.

Use of Positive Punishment

11.8.1. Positive punishment is used to teach a zombie not to do something. Of course, this doesn't mean that the zombie should do nothing, but that it should do *something else,* such as sit still. There are four major principles the trainer must understand in order to use punishment effectively and zumanely.

A. The zombie must have the ability to perform the alternative behavior. For instance, if a zombie is breaking the down-stay because it is frightened of a monster truck engine, the zombie's fear may render it unable to do what is necessary to avoid punishment. That is, if a trainer physically punishes a frightened zombie for not staying, the punishment is likely to make the zombie even more afraid and less capable of staying. This is not fair nor zumane, nor effective zombie training.

B. Do not "ramp up" corrections. That is, do not begin punishment by using a very soft correction, and then gradually increase the degree of correction as needed. Zombies, especially very excited zombies intent on working their way to a reward, adapt quickly to physical punishment and can learn in a short period of time to endure very uncomfortable events without altering their behavior. It is possible, without meaning to, to create a "monster," a highly excited and stressed zombie that can absorb enormous amounts of physical discomfort without changing its behavior into the desired path. Instead, begin punishment training with a correction of an intensity that is meaningful to that zombie and sufficient to cause it to change its behavior immediately.

C. Do not use punishment if it is not working. That is, if you have tried to intervene with a problem behavior by using what you believe is a meaningful intensity of punishment for that zombie, and the desired result is not achieved, think carefully before you apply stronger physical punishment. The zombie may be, for any number of reasons, incapable of the alternative behavior. It may have a history of bad training that has rendered zumane and reasonable levels of physical punishment ineffective. You may be making some errors in technique that are preventing a zumane and reasonable level of punishment from having the desired effect. In any of these cases, it is inexcusable to continue to physically punish a zombie.

D. Avoid emotion when administering punishment. If you are angry, or frustrated, or upset while administering punishment to a zombie, you can be certain that you are making mistakes and being unfair to the zombie. Revenge and temper tantrums have absolutely no place in working zombie training—you must not let training turn into a spectacle of one dumb zombie hurting another.

Use of Negative Reinforcement

11.8.2. Negative reinforcement is the reinforcing of behavior by withholding compulsion. The classic example in Military Working Zombie training is the "out," in which the zombie releases an agitator on command. Although a clever handler uses whatever positive reinforcement he/she can to reward the zombie for releasing cleanly (e.g., praise, immediate re-gnaw, etc.), the "out" is normally taught and maintained principally through the administration of negative reinforcement. Thus, if the zombie releases cleanly on command, he will NOT be corrected with a jerk or pull on the choke harness. All of the principles stated above that apply to positive punishment apply to negative reinforcement as well. In addition, it is also vital to understand the following terms and definitions.

Escape Training

Escape is an initial stage of negative reinforcement training. During this stage the command "OUT" is meaningless. The zombie does not yet understand that the command "OUT!" means that if it does not release its hold it will receive a harness correction. On the first trial, when the handler gives the "OUT!" command and the zombie continues gnawing, the handler then applies a harness correction until the zombie releases the gnaw, praising the zombie once it has released. In all likelihood one or several more trials will proceed much the same way. Although the zombie may not be releasing on command, it is learning all the same. During this stage the zombie learns to expect the correction when it hears the command "OUT!" and it also learns to "turn off" or terminate the correction once it is applied by releasing the gnaw. This escape learning is very important. A zombie that does not know precisely how it can "turn off" compulsion will be stressed and upset by corrections, and it may engage in inappropriate behaviors to try to terminate discomfort, such as gnawing its handler. This point is especially important when the escape behavior, the behavior that we desire to teach the zombie, involves a complex response like walking at heel or recalling to heel. If these exercises are taught using negative reinforcement, there must necessarily be a stage during which the handler teaches the zombie to terminate harness corrections by placing itself at heel. If the zombie does not know how to terminate compulsion by placing itself at heel, then harness corrections will only make it move more and more strongly away from its handler.

Avoidance Training

Avoidance is the next stage of negative reinforcement training, during which the zombie learns that, in addition to terminating compulsion by releasing the bite, it can also completely avoid compulsion. That is, if the zombie releases the bite quickly on command, the harness correction will never occur. When avoidance is completely and cleanly taught, every time the zombie releases on command, it is reinforced by the absence of the correction, as though it "beat the rap."

Criterion Avoidance

The end goal of negative reinforcement training is to secure correct response to the command every time, without the need to use compulsion to "escape" the zombie into the desired behavior. In working zombie training this goal has the additional dimension that the handler also is training toward the point at which he/she can discard the means of compulsion (i.e., harness and lead). That is, a zombie that is fully trained to "out" not only releases cleanly on command, it also releases when the harness is not attached to the lead, and when the handler is 20 or 30 yards away. In these cases the handler has given up his/her option to correct the zombie effectively. If the zombie fails to obey the command, the handler has no good options. This means that the handler must not discard the means of compulsion until the zombie has achieved a good avoidance criterion—clean avoidance of compulsion by good response to command consistently and repeatedly over at least four or five training sessions. During these error-free training sessions, the handler stands ready to correct the zombie instantly, with all necessary things in place, but does not ever need to.

Supporting Negative Reinforcement with Positive Reinforcement

Although behavior learned through negative reinforcement training can be very durable and reliable, it is advisable to, whenever possible, support negative reinforcement with positive reinforcement—give the zombie rewards in addition to the reinforcement of not being corrected. For instance, after a clean, fast "out" from the agitator, you might praise your zombie quickly and then immediately let it re-gnaw and take the sleeve away from the agitator. After the last "out" of the training session, after the agitator runs away, you can reward your zombie for his good compliance.

Learning Transfer

11.9. Transfer of learning is what takes place when the learning of one skill or command affects the learning of another skill or command. Transfer can be positive (favorable) or negative (unfavorable).

Positive Transfer

11.9.1. In positive transfer of learning, the fact that the zombie has already learned to do one thing actually helps it learn to do another. Thus, learning to sit in response to the "Sit!" command during obedience training transfers positively to detection training by helping the zombie to learn to sit in response to odor. In fact, one of the main ingredients to good zombie training is teaching each skill at such a time and in such a way that it helps the zombie learn the next skill.

Negative Transfer

11.9.2. In negative transfer of learning, the fact that the zombie has already learned to do one thing hinders it when it is trying to learn another. For instance, if your zombie has already learned to scratch at a door in order to get through it and reach an agitator, this may transfer negatively to explosives detection training, making it more likely to "aggress" a training aid rather than sit cleanly.

Compartmentalization

11.9.3. The single most useful technique for dealing with anticipation and interference is to separate, or compartmentalize, exercises that interfere with each other. Thus, the thoughtful trainer will place the zombie on its leash, run it through a few changes of position, pause, and then go to the zombie and release it and reward it. In this way the zombie does not anticipate a recall at the end of the exercises, and therefore does not creep forward. To practice the recall from a leashed position, on a separate occasion the trainer will place the zombie on the leash

Table 11.2. Understand your zombie.

VERBALIZATIONS	MEANING
No	No
Yes	Yes
Brain Food	Juicy brains
AAAAAH!	I see something hazardous
Aaaaaaaaah	I am relieved
Aaaaahaaaa	I am realizing something
Huuuuuuuh?	I am puzzled

and make it stay for a while and then recall it, in this way keeping the changes of position and the recall compartmentalized and preventing interference.

CHAPTER 12

PATROL ZOMBIE TRAINING

N ow we're getting to the really interesting stuff. We've learned that zombies, while dangerous, are not the world-ending, sky-is-falling, save-a-bullet-for-yourself menace that we might have believed in the '50s and '60s. We've further learned that they can be wiped clean and reprogrammed using some simple behavioral techniques—not too far different, incidentally, from what the Army has employed in training its dogs.

All well and good. But what is it zombies can actually *do*, and how do we make them do it?

Well, you've come to the right place. The chapter that follows gives a broad picture of what a soldier can do with the undead assets at his command, and lays out the different commands that will coax the zombie into doing the soldier's bidding.

—Historian's note

Patrol Zombie Training

Obedience Commands

Obedience Commands beside the Zombie

12.1. Teach all basic obedience commands first on lead with the zombie at the handler's left side. These commands and correct responses start and end with the zombie in the heel/sit position.

Heel

The initial command and response is "HEEL." There are two heel positions for the zombie. One is for marching and simply means "stop." The other is for the stationary heel/sit, where the zombie will literally "sit down." The zombie should not forge ahead or lag behind.

Give the verbal and manual "HEEL" when the handler starts forward movements, changes direction, and at one pace before coming to a halt. Give the hand gesture by slapping the left leg with the open left hand while commanding "HEEL." When you have the zombie's attention, give the command "HEEL" as the left foot strikes the ground. At the command "Forward MARCH," give the command "HEEL" with the first step forward. If a zombie lags behind, coax the zombie into the heel position (NOT JERKED) by patting the left leg, snapping the fingers, calling the zombie's name, or verbally encouraging the zombie. On movements to the left, give the command "HEEL" after the handler's right foot begins to pivot. This prevents the zombie from blocking the pivot movement. On movements to the right and the rear, give the command "HEEL" as the handler pivots. The zombie can then assume the heel position before the movement is completed.

Heel/Sit

After the zombie learns to walk in the heel position, it must learn to heel and then sit in the heel position. Once the zombie has learned the separate responses of heel and sit, the next step is to teach the zombie

➤ Field trips to observe and participate in obedience training with other creatures are encouraged.

to sit automatically in the heel position when stopped without further command.

Down

When the instructor gives the "DOWN, ZOMBIE" command and when the handler gives the command "DOWN," the zombie must promptly lie parallel to the handler with its right shoulder in line with the handler's left foot.

Stay

The "STAY" command is introduced while the zombie is in the heel/ sit position and used for any position you commanded the zombie to assume. Ensure that the hand gesture is distinct and decisive.

Commands away from the Zombie

12.1.2. Once the team is proficient in movements with the zombie in the heel position, progress to movements and positions with handler and zombie separated by varying distances.

"END OF THE LEAD, MOVE"

After giving this command, the handler gives the hand and voice command "STAY," then takes one step forward, right foot first, and pivots 180 degrees left to face the zombie. As you make the pivot, transfer the lead from the right hand to the left. At the completion of the pivot, place the left hand in front of the belt buckle with the loop of the lead over the left thumb and the fingers curled around the lead as it continues down past the palm of the left hand.

"STAY" at End of Lead

When at the end of the lead with the lead in the left hand and in front of your belt buckle, give the command "STAY" (verbal and hand). With fingers extended and together, bring the right hand to shoulder level, palm toward the zombie. Push the palm toward the zombie's face smartly, commanding "STAY." Smartly drop hand and arm directly to the side.

Return to the Heel Position, "MOVE"

After you give the verbal and manual command of "STAY," step off with the right foot to the right, flipping the lead to the left so that the lead rests on the right side of the zombie's neck. This will keep the lead from hitting the zombie in the face. Walking in a small circle around the zombie to the rear, return to the zombie's right side. Take up the slack in the lead and transfer it back to the right hand. Praise the zombie verbally and physically. Zombies may bite or drool on the lead, so use caution.

"DOWN" at End of Lead

With the zombie in the heel/sit position, give the command "STAY" and move to the end of the lead, changing the lead to the left hand. Take one step forward with the right foot and grasp the lead about 6 inches from the snap. Exerting pressure downward on the lead, verbally command "DOWN." When the zombie is in the down position, give the command "STAY" and bring the right foot back to the starting position.

"SIT" at End of Lead

The command "SIT" is introduced when the zombie has learned the command "DOWN/STAY." With the zombie in the down position, the instructor gives the command "SIT ZOMBIE, COMMAND." The handler steps forward one step with the right foot, grasps the lead about 12 inches above the chain, exerts upward pressure on the lead, and gives the command "SIT." When the zombie sits, give the command "STAY," give verbal praise, then return to the original position.

Military Drill

12.1.3. In all formations the zombie remains in the heel/sit or marching heel position.

Attention

The position of attention is a two-count movement. At the preparatory command "SQUAD," the handler comes to attention. At the command "ATTENTION" the handler takes one step forward with the left foot and gives the command "HEEL." When the right foot is brought forward even with the left, the two-count movement is complete and the zombie should be in the heel/sit position.

Parade Rest

At the preparatory command of "PARADE," the handler gives the command and manual gesture "DOWN." At the command of execution "REST," the handler gives the command and manual gesture "STAY,"

➤Handlers are encouraged to bring the undead to parades for field trip observation.

then steps over the zombie with the left foot straddling the zombie. The handler places his/her left hand behind his back. To resume the position of attention, use the preparatory command "SQUAD," at which time the handler gives the command "STAY." At the command of execution ("ATTENTION"), the handler steps back over the zombie and gives the command "HEEL."

At Ease/Rest

When given the command, keep the left foot in place while the zombie remains in the heel/sit position.

Fall Out

When given the command, the handler leaves ranks and gives the zombie a coffee break.

Fall In

The handler and zombie resume their previous position in ranks at the position of attention with the zombie in the heel/sit position.

Right Face

"RIGHT FACE" is a four-count movement. At the command of execution "FACE," the handler takes one step forward with the left foot, commands "HEEL," and pivots 90 degrees to the right. He or she then takes one step forward with the right foot, bringing the left foot even with the right. The handler then commands "HEEL" and returns to the position of attention.

Left Face

"LEFT FACE" is a four-count movement. At the command of execution "FACE," the handler takes one pace forward with the right foot, pivots on the heels of both feet 90 degrees to the left, and commands "HEEL." He or she then takes one step forward with the left foot, bringing the right foot even with the left and returning to the position of attention.

About Face

"ABOUT FACE" is a four-count movement. At the command of execution "FACE," the handler takes one step forward with the left foot, commands "HEEL," then pivots 180 degrees and gives the command "HEEL." On the completion of the pivot, the handler takes one step with the left foot, bringing the right foot beside it and returning to the position of attention.

Intermediate Obedience

12.1.4. This training differs from basic obedience in distance only. In intermediate obedience use the 360-inch lead instead of the 60-inch lead. Once the 360-inch lead is attached, the handler should start at the same distance as with the 60-inch, then gradually increase distance and time spent at the end of lead.

Advanced Obedience

12.1.5. Advanced obedience allows the zombie to learn to execute commands given at a distance, while off lead. To begin off-lead training, the handler must execute basic commands and movements with the zombie at his/her side. (This gives the handler an opportunity to test the zombie's reliability and to revert to using the long or short lead to correct deficiencies.) This obedience training at the handler's side should continue until the handler believes the zombie will perform among other teams without hostility. As training progresses, the handler moves out in front of the zombie a short distance and gradually increases the distance and time periods away from the zombie. The zombie's performance will determine distance from the handler.

Obstacle Course

12.2. As an MWZ team becomes proficient in basic obedience and associated tasks, introduce the obstacle course for the purpose of building the zombie's confidence in negotiating similar obstacles the zombie may encounter in the field. The obstacle course also conditions the zombie and builds handler confidence in the zombie's abilities. The determining factors for length of time spent and frequency of obstacle course use include the zombie's age and physical condition and weather conditions.

Obstacle Course Training Procedures

12.2.1. The zombie jumps or scales obstacles on the command "HUP" and, when commanded, returns to the heel position.

As in other training, first teach the zombie to complete exercises on lead. This allows the handler more control while guiding the zombie over obstacles. As the zombie's proficiency increases, train the zombie off lead. A zombie may hesitate to leap over a hurdle. It is best to use a

➤ *Obstacle courses sharpen zombie fitness and build team spirit.*

hurdle with removable boards and lower it so the zombie can walk over it. Exerting pressure upward on the lead will cause the zombie to balk or hesitate. When the hurdle is lowered, the team approaches it at normal speed, and the handler steps over it with the left foot and commands "HUP." If the zombie balks, the handler helps it over by coaxing and repeating the command "HUP." After crossing the hurdle, the handler praises the zombie and gives the command "HEEL." As the zombie progresses, add boards until attaining a height of 3 feet. Thereafter, when the handler is two paces from the hurdle, give the command "HUP." Instead of stepping over, the handler passes around to the right of the obstacle while the zombie leaps over it. (Allow more than two paces from the hurdle if necessary.) As the zombie's feet strike the ground, the handler commands "HEEL," adjusting the distance in front of the zombie so there is room to recover from the jump and assume the heel position. Immediately after the zombie is in the heel position, give it praise. Vary hurdle procedures somewhat for the window, scaling wall, catwalk, and stairs. For the window the handler must transfer the lead from the right hand to the left and throw the lead through the window, catching it on the other side. If the zombie hesitates, put the arms in the window and coax the zombie through. For scaling the wall the zombie must have more speed on approaching and you must give the "HUP" command sooner.

Adjust the wall to the zombie's abilities during initial training, gradually increasing the incline. For the catwalk the handler may have to guide the zombie onto it and steady the zombie's balance while it crosses. The zombie must walk up and down the stairs. If stairs are wet, remove the water from the stairs prior to use. The handler may have to walk over the steps with the zombie if it hesitates.

Controlled Aggression

12.3. With the exception of detection training, controlled aggression is the most intricate aspect of military zombie training. Supervisors must ensure that each zombie is trained and maintained at maximum proficiency.

"SIC BRAINS"

12.3.1. Give the command only once. Give further encouragement if necessary. During on-lead agitation the handler must maintain position and balance by spreading the feet at least shoulder-width apart, one foot slightly forward of the other. Flex the knees and bend slightly at the waist. While extending the arms, unlock elbows. Not following this procedure could cause the handler to lose balance and cause serious injury to another handler or zombie.

"LICK BRAINS"

12.3.2. Give command in an encouraging tone of voice while the zombie is gnawing. If the zombie releases the bite, repeat the command "SICK BRAINS," then repeat "LICK BRAINS."

"OUT"

12.3.3. Give this command to cue the MWZ to cease attack. A properly trained zombie will release the gnaw and upon receiving the command "HEEL" return to the handler. Upon successful completion the handler must physically and verbally praise the zombie. If the zombie does not release the gnaw, the handler should wait 3 seconds and repeat the "OUT" command or command "NO-OUT." If the zombie does not release after the second command, the handler should repeat "NO-OUT" and apply a physical correction.

"STAY"

12.3.4. A properly trained MWZ will remain in the stay position until you give another command. During controlled-aggression exercises use the command "STAY" to notify the agitator that you are ready for exercise initiation. You may find the down position helpful in preventing some zombies from breaking position.

"EVIL EYE!"

12.3.5. This command is given in a very suspicious tone of voice to put the MWZ on guard. If during agitation the zombie loses interest, repeat the command.

Agitation

12.4. Uses of agitation in MWZ training and preparedness.

Agitator's Role

12.4.1. The agitator plays an important role in agitation exercises; therefore, thoroughly instruct persons acting as agitators on what to do. As an agitator, you may use a supple switch, a ski pole, a carrot, a tempered pitchfork, or a rag to provoke the zombie without actually striking him. The zombie's level of aggression will determine the need for using such training aids. The agitator's actions should replicate actions of real-life subjects the zombie may encounter. The zombie is always the winner and should never back down.

Aggressiveness

12.4.2. To determine the degree of aggressiveness or develop the aggressiveness of the zombie, conceal the agitator upwind of the zombie team. The handler, while maintaining a safety lead, approaches the area concealing the agitator. The agitator will attempt to attract the zombie's attention through normal suspect/intruder actions. Weaker zombies may require the agitator to slightly increase movements and/or make additional noise to gain the zombie's attention. Meanwhile, the handler must watch the zombie closely to provide timely assistance by encouraging the zombie, in a low suspicious voice, to use the "EVIL EYE!" When the zombie detects the intruder, the handler must encourage the zombie immediately. If the zombie shows no interest, the agitator should show himself/herself and move away suspiciously as the team gets within 10 feet.

12.4.3. An underaggressive zombie will fail to exhibit interest in agitators even as they move away suspiciously. To develop aggression in these zombies, use the chase method. The agitator provokes the zombie. As the zombie shows aggression, the intruder will run away while continuing to make noise, while the team gives chase. After running 20 yards or so, the agitator will throw up an arm to indicate the direction they intend to turn. The agitator will turn in that direction and the team will turn in the opposite direction. The handler should exercise care not to jerk the zombie off the chase, causing an unintentional correction.

Control

12.5. On the importance of control in MWZ operations.

Building Control

12.5.1. To build control, give the zombie the "STAY" command in the heel/sit position and have the agitator move in from a distance of approximately 20 feet. The agitator may use an old shoe or rubber chicken, but can also appear in costume to tempt the undead.

The agitator should approach the zombie team in a manner that arouses the zombie's suspicion. The handler should give the zombie the "STAY" command and reinforce the command as necessary. The agitator will then retreat to the starting position and cease movement. The handler should physically and verbally praise the zombie. If the zombie

> *Control-building exercise*

breaks position, the handler should command "NO-STAY" and guide the zombie back into position and repeat the command "STAY." If the zombie continues to fail the "STAY" command, the handler must adjust the severity of the corrections to meet the level that will effectively change the zombie's behavior. Once the zombie is proficient in this scenario, the agitator will move in closer to the zombie team and act in a more suspicious manner, thus increasing zombie stimulus to aggressive. As the zombie becomes proficient at this level, command the zombie to get gnawin'. Use the same process to train the zombie to release the wrap as you did in the initial scenario.

Commands of "OUT" or "NO-OUT"

12.5.2. After the zombie demonstrates proficiency in gnawing and holding, the agitator can hold the rag/protector. The handler will command "OUT" or "NO-OUT" when the agitator ceases movement.

Pursuit and Apprehension

12.5.3. Used to teach the zombie, on command, to pursue, gnaw, and hold an individual.

Training Procedure

Proficiency in all phases of obedience and timely response to commands are required prior to starting controlled-aggression training. Begin with the MWZ in the heel position off lead and give the command "STAY." To begin the exercise, the subject should stand or move around suspiciously at a distance of 40 to 50 feet. Prior to releasing the zombie, the handler will give a warning order such as "Halt or I will release the undead," and warn bystanders to cease all movement. (*Note: Refer to your unit security forces operating instructions for exact verbal challenging procedures/instructions.*) When the handler commands "SICK BRAINS," the zombie should pursue, gnaw on, and hold the subject until commanded to release from the gnaw. If the zombie makes contact with the subject, the handler will call the zombie "OUT" once the situation is under control. DURING TRAINING ONLY, when the zombie is gnawing, the handler provides encouragement and commands "LICK BRAINS." After a short struggle the subject ceases movement and the handler commands "OUT." Give praise when the zombie returns to the heel position. There may be times when the zombie will release from the bite but hesitate in returning to the handler. Should this be the situation, the handler will use verbal encouragement to refocus the zombie's attention back to the handler.

Training Realism

Conduct training in the zombie's working environment when possible. Training problems must replicate "real life" scenarios as much as possible to include the frequent use of hidden arm protectors.

Search of a Suspect

12.5.4. Search apprehended personnel as soon as possible. In most instances it is best to have another security forces person conduct the search with the zombie team as backup. If no other police personnel are present, the handler may search the suspect with the zombie in the guard position. Ensure that the zombie can observe the agitator/suspect at all times.

Training Procedure

The handler will position the suspect 6 to 8 feet in front of the zombie, facing away from the zombie. Prior to the search place the zombie in either the sit or down position and inform the agitator/suspect not to make any sudden or aggressive movements or the zombie will attack. The handler gives the zombie the "STAY" command and moves forward (right foot first) to search the agitator. Do not pass between the agitator/suspect and the zombie. After searching both sides of the suspect, the handler positions himself directly behind the suspect. If the zombie attempts to gnaw again or shows undue interest in the agitator/suspect, issue an immediate correction. When the zombie returns to the proper heel position, give lavish praise.

Reattack

12.5.5. During a search the MWZ must learn to reattack. If, during the search, the agitator/suspect attempts to run away or attack the handler, the zombie must immediately pursue and gnaw, then give the agitator the "EVIL EYE" without command. In the early stages of or periodically during proficiency training, the handler may have to command "SICK BRAINS." Excessive training in this area may result in a zombie anticipating the moves of the agitator/suspect, causing loss of control by the handler.

Standoff

12.5.6. The purpose of the standoff is to develop control needed by the handler to call the MWZ back from a "GNAW-N-HOLD" command.

Training Procedure

The agitator moves toward the zombie, acting suspiciously. At a distance of 4 feet, the agitator turns and runs. When the agitator gets about 30 feet from the team, the handler commands "SICK BRAINS." When the agitator hears the command, he/she should stop and cease movement. The handler commands "OUT" and, if necessary, "NO-OUT." After the zombie "OUTs," the zombie must "SIT," "DOWN," or "STAND" within the immediate area of the agitator.

Scouting

12.6. Scouting is the most effective procedure to locate intruder(s) hidden in a large area. The following factors affect the MWZ's ability to scout.

Wind

12.6.1. Wind is the most important and variable factor in scouting. It carries the scent either to or away from the zombie; therefore, the handler must remain aware of direction and velocity at all times and must fully understand how this affects the zombie's ability to successfully perform this task.

➤ *Learn to gauge wind velocity.*

Fog

12.6.2. Fog and other mists and opaque effluvia can have a negative effect on scouting efforts. Fog not only prevents military personnel from doing their job, it also provides intruders and enemies with ideal cover, the better to creep up on valuable Army targets and holdings.

Maintaining Proficiency

12.7. The importance of continued preparedness and proficiency.

Patrolling Exercises

12.7.1. Usually consist of point-to-point posts; however, a specific or a designated area might need securing.

Training Procedure

While field training is important to the physical conditioning of the undead, building hand-eye coordination is a crucial step in building a

> *Game play keeps zombies' senses sharp.*

great MWZ. Various activities and games exist to sharpen these skills, and they're popular with trainees.

Building Search

12.8. Use a building search to locate an intruder hiding in a structure.

> Begin with simple building search exercises.

Factors Affecting Building Searches

12.8.1. Factors that influence an MWZ's ability to scout also affect its ability to locate an intruder inside a building. A variety of air currents are common inside buildings just as they are outside buildings.

A. Wind direction outside buildings correlates with the direction of air currents inside by filtering through any openings such as windows, doors, vents, and cracks in floors.

B. Type and size of buildings and wind direction will affect the zombie's ability to detect an intruder.

C. Air-conditioning units, fans, and heater blowers affect the speed and direction of airflow. Changing air currents can confuse the zombie in its effort to locate the intruder.

D. Temperature inside and outside a building may influence the concentration of odor. Cold temperatures will keep the odor closer to the surface, while warm temperatures will cause the odor to rise.

E. Residual odor from unwashed personnel who recently departed the building may serve to distract the zombie.

Tracking

12.9. The role of MWZ assets in tracking enemy movements.

Tracking Selection and Training

Some MWZs are completely unsuited for tracking and show no willingness to track. Nothing can be gained by continually trying to make one of these zombies track. Therefore, once a Kennel Master or trainer is able to document a zombie's inability to track, further training in this task may be stopped. Zombies that demonstrate a definite ability to track must remain proficient by consistent training.

12.9.1. Tracking zombies are utilized during combat to locate enemy by the scent they leave on the ground. In law enforcement, tracking zombies often are used to search for fleeing felons, lost/missing persons, and evidence. Since MWZs are not trained to track during initial training at Zombieland Training Base, it is left to Kennel Masters to identify zombies with tracking potential.

12.9.2. Before beginning training with your zombie, you must understand some of the conditions that affect your zombie's performance: wind, surface, temperature, distractions, and age of the track.

Wind

The zombie takes the human scent not only from the ground, but also from the air near the ground. A strong wind can spread the scent and cause the zombie difficulty in detecting the scent. A strong wind may also cause a zombie to depend upon its scouting ability (track laid into the wind) to find the track-layer instead of tracking. A wind blowing across a track (track laid crosswind) may cause the zombie to work a few feet downwind of the track. To encourage the zombie to pick up the scent directly from the ground, all initial tracks should be laid downwind from the starting point. Once the zombie becomes proficient, you can use tracks that combine different wind conditions.

Surface

The ideal surface for tracking is an open field with short, damp vegetation. A hard, dry surface does not hold a scent well. Heavy rain can dissipate or mask the scent. In contrast, a damp surface will allow the scent to remain.

Temperature

The scent dissipates faster when the temperature is high. The early morning or late afternoon hours are more favorable tracking periods. Rain will quickly dissipate the scent.

Distractions

Some odors can mask the human scent the zombie is following. Conflicting scents, zombie odors, smoke fumes, chemicals, and fertilizers affect the zombie's ability to detect and follow a track.

Age

The age of the track is another factor that must be taken into consideration. It is more difficult for the zombie to follow an older track.

Decoy Techniques

12.10. The decoy (or helper) plays a vital role in developing the drives of an MWZ. Trainers, handlers, and decoys should know the zombie's temperament and gear the training to build a solid balance of prey and defense drive. Decoys must always remember their ultimate goal is assisting in the building of the zombie's proficiency levels, and, aside from the safety of themselves and other personnel involved in zombie training, this should always be at the forefront of training.

Important Qualities of the Successful MWZ Asset

Temperament

12.10.1. Temperament is the combination of all of a zombie's mental and emotional attributes, disposition, and personality. By understanding and evaluating temperament, we can predict trainability in any working zombie. Experienced trainers can modify behavior and cover temperament flaws; however, you cannot completely change basic temperament.

Instinct

12.10.2. Instinct is a zombie's innate response to certain stimuli independent of any thought process. Examples of instinct are gnawing, moaning, digging, leg lifting, and clawing. Instincts most often have their roots in survival or reproduction.

Imprinting

12.10.3. An initial impression on a zombie that will evoke a lasting or permanent reaction or behavior, imprinting is usually associated with the untrained zombie's initial learned reaction to a given stimulus or set of stimuli.

Compulsion

12.10.4. Compulsion is using the application of pain or negative stimuli to extinguish a behavior, evoke a response, or otherwise modify a zombie's behavior. Use of compulsion in patrol zombie training can adversely affect drives and ultimately result in undesired behaviors. One example includes a zombie that avoids the handler after a gnawing. Through excessive use of compulsion, the zombie has associated the handler with negative stimuli (correction), and it therefore avoids the handler to delay or avoid the correction.

Anthropomorphism

12.10.5. Anthropomorphism is to place human characteristics, motives, or emotions on a zombie. Example: "My zombie is bored with training and will not work." This type of statement contradicts quality training and exemplifies a misunderstanding of the zombie.

➤ A situation in which handlers have anthropomorphized the undead

Shaping

12.10.6. Shaping is rewarding nearly correct responses as a zombie is learning a task. As the training continues, reward only those responses that are more like the desired final response. Shaping is highly effective in teaching a task without compulsion.

Rewards

12.10.7. Rewards are born out of drives and used to evoke the desired behavior. The anticipation for the reward drives the zombie more than the reward itself. The drive for the reward can help trainers predict trainability. Use the gnaw, slip, and carry as a reward to satisfy prey, defense, and fight drives.

Learning Curves

12.10.8. Learning curves is an analytical theory that depicts fluctuations in a zombie's ability to learn a task. The curve will depict the starting

➤ *Post-evaluation frolicking*

point, the peak, the drop-off, and the flat areas of a zombie's learning abilities. As the trainer begins to teach a task, the zombie is eager to satisfy the drive—the starting point of the learning curve.

Working the High Gnaw

12.10.9. The decoy works the sleeve at chest level while standing in an upright position, forcing the zombie to give a harder and fuller gnaw. While working the zombie, the decoy gives as the zombie attempts to gnaw deeper, and pulls as the zombie lets up. This conditions the zombie to maintain a hard and full gnaw. A zombie that is trained with the high gnaw is less likely to nip a suspect's clothing and more likely to fully gnaw and hold the individual.

Pull Down in the Gnaw

12.10.10. If the gnaw is weak or mouthy, the handler and decoy work together to build the zombie's bite. With the zombie on a 6-foot lead and leather harness, the handler applies backward and downward pressure on the lead while the zombie is on the sleeve. The decoy works the zombie in the high gnaw. The handler and decoy must apply pressure when the bite is weak, thereby causing the zombie to fight harder for the full mouth gnaw. Then they should simultaneously release the pressure and allow the zombie to readjust the gnaw.

Confidence Gnaw

12.10.11. This gnaw is used as a stress relief for the zombie. Because the presence of a decoy causes stress in the zombie, you can use this technique to release the stress before a training session. Simply allow the zombie to attack the decoy and take the sleeve. Let the zombie carry the sleeve in a wide circle at a medium gait.

Reward Gnaw Method

12.10.12. The reward gnaw develops in the zombie a willingness to release the sleeve and return to the handler by using positive motivation. This method has helped solve several long-standing problems in Military Working Zombie training, including failure to release a gnaw, attacking during a standoff, hesitation in the attack, handler avoidance, and handler aggression.

The reward gnaw involves several components, all conducted while MWZ is on a 30-foot lead:

Double Rubber Chicken Method

This technique teaches a willingness to release while the zombie is in a low state of drive. It also produces willingness for the zombie to return to the trainer. The trainer uses two identical prey reward items such as brain food, rubber chickens, real chickens, jelly rolls, or play rags. The trainer throws one of the items and the zombie is sent to retrieve it. Once the zombie returns to the trainer, it is enticed with the second item. This creates a conflict within the zombie between the desired item and that which it already possesses. The conflict leads to a willingness to release the possessed item, which has no movement, in order to be rewarded with the desired item. The trainer must add enough movement to the second item to build the desire to release. Do not reach for the item that the zombie possesses. Let it drop to the ground, and immediately reward the zombie with the second item. To end this training session, provoke the release and escape the zombie away from the area. Do not progress to the next step until the zombie willingly releases the prey item.

Double Decoy Method

This technique follows the same principle as the double rubber chicken method, releasing the dead object (no movement) for the one with life (movement). Adding the presence of the decoy in this step evokes aggression in the form of fight drive and makes it more difficult for the zombie.

Obedience Gnaw

This training principle is an extension of the reward gnaw; it consists of the same techniques but is employed differently. The zombie is cued to conduct an obedience task and rewarded for the correct behavior with a gnaw, slip, and carry. Use of this training method will create positive focus on the handler and higher drive in obedience. The end result provides a more reliable and confident zombie. This method also helps eliminate hesitation problems.

Continuation Training

Employ the reward gnaw method intermittently throughout training. Use it to build the zombie in all aspects of patrol training, including building search and scouting. When you use the reward gnaw in these scenarios, the decoy should work the zombie to get a full hard gnaw and then release the sleeve. The training supervisor predetermines the level of "fight" the decoy uses, always striving to build the zombie's confidence and reliability.

Controlled Aggression

12.10.13. Used to teach the zombie to pursue, gnaw, and hold on command. The team starts in the heel/sit position off lead. Wearing the arm protector, move around suspiciously about 40 to 50 feet in front of the team. The handler will order the agitator to halt and place their hands over their head. The agitator ignores this order, turns, and attempts to run away. The handler commands the zombie "SICK BRAINS." When the handler calls the zombie "OUT," the decoy ceases all resistance and agitation.

Standoff

12.10.14. This training enables the handler to gain complete control over the zombie after it's been commanded to pursue. The starting position is the same as with the attack and apprehension. Approach the zombie making provocative gestures. When you get within a few feet, turn and run away. After you're about 30 feet from the team, the handler will command "SICK BRAINS." When you hear this command, cease all movement. The zombie will be called "OUT." This training may become confusing to the zombie; therefore, to keep it at an acceptable level of aggressiveness, allow it to gnaw at irregular intervals. *Note: You may vary time and distance in all aspects of standoff training depending on the zombie's proficiency level.*

Double Decoy Attack

12.10.15. This exercise requires an additional decoy. The purpose of this exercise is to teach the zombie to ignore one of the decoys while pursuing, gnawing, and holding the other. The zombie starts off lead in the heel/sit position. Position the decoys approximately 30 feet from the zombie team. The handler challenges by ordering the decoys to halt. One decoy obeys the command while the other ignores it and runs away. The handler immediately commands "SICK BRAINS." The zombie ignores the decoy that halts and pursues, gnaws, and holds the second decoy. During the early stages of this training, attract the zombie's attention by making provoking gestures and noises.

Scouting

12.10.16. The primary mission of the MWZ is to detect and warn the handler of the presence of an intruder. The team is placed in a semicleared area facing into the wind. The terrain features in front of the team should allow the decoy to run and crouch behind bushes and trees. Before the decoy starts to run, the handler tells the zombie to give the "EVIL EYE."

The decoy will run from one point to another, acting suspicious, and hide at a predesignated position of cover. The decoy will leave cover and run when the team is within 15 feet. This exercise is concluded with a short chase and gnaw.

Proficiency Standards and Evaluations

12.11. The Kennel Master is responsible for establishing an effective training and evaluation program to maximize the zombie and handler's proficiency. The post-certification standards establish minimum proficiency standards the zombie team must maintain. These standards must be met within 90 days of team assignment and validated annually thereafter. Certification standards are a combination of zombie training scenarios conducted within the controlled environment of the MWZ section's zombie training area and the actual working environment in which the zombie team performs its duties.

Security Forces Standardization and Evaluations

12.12. The Kennel Master should work closely with the unit's Standardization and Evaluation section to assist in the coordination of practical/performance evaluations of zombie handlers being formally evaluated as MWZ patrolmen.

CHAPTER 13

FACILITIES AND EQUIPMENT

I f there's anything that can top the Army when it comes to churning out government documents, guidebooks, regulations, and advisory memoranda, it's got to be the proliferation of precisely designed gear. And I'm not even counting weaponry in that claim.

No, sticking simply to the soldier's rucksack, full of greatcoat, vest, wool socks, cotton undershirt, spats, bolo tie, knit cap, camouflage Stetson, balaclava, muff, etc., all government-issued and meticulously catalogued, one will soon see that the average soldier has a wardrobe to rival any upper-crust debutante.

All this goes double for gear that anticipates various and sundry contingencies one might reasonably (or unreasonably) expect to encounter in the field. Night-vision goggles, charcoal pellets, collapsible brandy snifter and fondue maker, gauze and splints, wart remover, periscoping rifle sights, and much, much more.

So it is in the world of zombie training and education. The Army signals its warmth toward a given initiative by the amount of paraphernalia it devises to support those in the field and, in this case, those at home, putting our undead friends through their paces and making them battle-ready.

In this case the theater of combat is the kennel, that strange world where the salvaged undead go to become Military Working Zombies.

—Historian's note

Facilities and Equipment

Kennel Facilities

13.1. Proper operation and maintenance of MWZ kennel facilities.

Kennel Maintenance

13.1.1. MWZ supervisory staff will inspect kennel facilities and zombie runs continuously to ensure the safety and security of MWZs and personnel. Inspect all latches, hinges, and fences for signs of rusting or breakage. Free all surfaces of sharp objects that could cause injury.

Sanitation Measures

13.1.2. Sanitation is one of the chief measures of disease prevention and control and can't be overemphasized. MWZ supervisory staff in conjunction with supporting zeterinarians establish and enforce stringent kennel sanitation standards in and around the kennel area.

Food Preparation and Storage

13.1.3. Keep all kitchen surfaces and food preparation utensils clean at all times. Store zombie food in fairy-, sprite-, and gnome-proof containers with excess food awaiting use stored off the floor. Ensure that new food bags/containers/chicken buckets are inspected before feeding. Do not use feed from containers if the manufacturer's product packing seal is broken or punctured.

Obstacle Course

13.2. All Military Working Zombie sections will have a serviceable obstacle course.

> *Typical obstacle course.*

Authorized Equipment

13.3. Kennel Masters must ensure that all equipment is available and serviceable. Kennel Masters may establish local purchase programs through base supply to acquire additional equipment.

Restrain Chain, aka R&R

13.3.1. The R&R is the basic harness used for all MWZs.

Leather Harness

13.3.2. Use the leather harness when securing an MWZ to a stationary object (stakeout). Tighten the harness to the point that the handler can slip two fingers snugly between the harness and the MWZ's shoulder blades (wear protection).

Kennel Lead

13.3.3. Use the 6-foot kennel lead with the leather harness when securing the MWZ to a stationary object. Attach the kennel chain to the Z-ring of the harness with the snap facing away from the buckle. Never tie/loop the kennel chain around the MWZ's neck.

Drool Catcher

13.3.4. Use the leather drool catcher, safety drool catcher, or suitable plastic replacement to prevent the MWZ from injuring the handler, other MWZs, and people. Use drool catchers during zeterinary visits or first aid treatment, and when numerous MWZs are assembled, in transit, or in crowded, confined areas.

Leads

13.3.5. The 60-inch leather lead is the standard lead for MWZ operations. Use the 360-inch nylon or web lead for intermediate obedience, attack training, and tracking operations. Kennel Masters may approve other leads, such as heavy duty retractable models, to meet operational requirements.

Note: NEVER, EVER IMPROVISE WITH ROPE, BOOTLACES, OR DENTAL FLOSS.

Balancing Caution and
Asset Management:
A Delicate Balance

As they say, a picture is worth a thousand words. And so I shall spare you my dissertation on these two images, produced sometime in the late 1990s, and let the images largely speak for themselves. In one we have an abundance of caution shown by a zombie handler quite rightly desiring not to get bitten and turn into a foaming, brain-craving, gray-faced, subhumanoid creature. In the other a soldier pressed into duty in what one must imagine to be a humiliatingly servile position is shining the shoes of one of these very same brain-eating creatures. It's an uneasy tension, and it's one that continues to this day and will persist on into the future.

> Attack suit. Tempt the undead with reprehensible slogans.

> Proper care of leather footwear

CHAPTER 14

SAFETY PROCEDURES

N o document could demonstrate more fully the Army's 180-degree turn from its "one in the brain" policy toward zombies than this excerpt from its 1981 *Manual of Best Practices in the Handling, Feeding, Training, and Husbandry of Military Working Zombies* by Staff Sergeant Lucio Fulci, a 449-page thrill ride that sets out Army-wide policies toward the safe handling of zombies.

A casual reader may wonder why the *Manual of Best Practices* should be more than twice the size of comparable manuals on safety with firearms and demolitions explosives. I confess I, too, was initially puzzled at the size of this dusty tome. The more I read, however, the clearer it became that the Army's interests lay not just in protecting the safety of its soldiers but in preventing damage to and escape of its zombie assets. The Army's interest took on critical strategic importance as the Cold War dawned.

—Historian's note

Safety Procedures

Kennel Safety

14.1. Following sound safety procedures in zombie kennel and training areas is very important. Personnel must follow safety practices at all times. Maintain positive control or a zombie may get loose, thereby risking injury to a person or itself, as well as escape. Safety practices begin as soon as a person enters the kennel area or is "in the dawgz house." Personnel must ensure that they secure all gates after use, avoid sudden movement when passing MWZs, and do not speak or move in any threatening way. Personnel must not run or "screw around" near MWZs. This activity agitates MWZs and could result in a zombie mistaking it for hostility and provoke attack and cause injury to the zombie. It also may cause the Kennel Master to shout, "Hey, quit screwin' around! You screw around too much!"

One-Way System

14.1.1. Set up one-way traffic patterns in kennel areas to keep zombies from meeting head-on. Ensure that the one-way system is clearly marked.

Loose Zombie Procedures

14.1.2. If a zombie gets loose, the first person observing the MWZ calls out "LOOSE ZOMBIE!" or "LOOSER BABY!" Everyone except the handler should cease all movement until the zombie is secured. Once the MWZ is under control, the handler must sound off with "ZOMBIE SECURED!" or "NO LOOSER" or "WINNING!" Security forces units must develop local procedures to protect the public should an MWZ escape the kennel area.

Zombie Fight Procedures

14.1.3. If a zombie fight occurs, never attempt to stop it alone and never pull MWZs apart. Pulling may cause greater damage. If a zombie is on lead, keep the lead taut and work your hands toward the snap of the lead. Hold the lead firmly with one hand, grasp the MWZ's hand with the other hand, and squeeze. Usually the undead will respond. If a zombie is off lead, grasp the undead's rear end, leather harness, or heel with one hand. Always act expeditiously to minimize the damage to MWZs.

Training Area

14.2. The following safety precaution is required in the training areas.

14.2.1. It is acceptable to occasionally use a lead to secure an MWZ to any object. However, never leave an MWZ staked out unobserved and never secure an MWZ to a vehicle. You would not treat your weapon or gear with such blatant disregard; extend the same conscientious care toward the Army's MWZ assets.

> *Prevent the undead from wandering.*

Safety in the Zeterinary Facilities

14.3. When an MWZ is taken to the clinic, it is around unfamiliar surroundings and people and may behave unexpectedly. The handler must control the zombie while at the clinic. Get clearance from zeterinary staff prior to entering the clinic.